SEEKING

SEEKING A LIFE THAT MATTERS

WISDOM FOR TODAY FROM THE BOOK OF PROVERBS

Katharine Dell

DARTON · LONGMAN + TODD

First published in 2002 by
Darton, Longman and Todd Ltd
1 Spencer Court
140–142 Wandsworth High Street
London SW18 4JJ

ISBN 0–232–52402–5

A catalogue record for this book is available from the British Library.

Designed by Sandie Boccacci
Phototypeset in 12.25/13.5pt Perpetua
by Intype London Ltd
Printed and bound in Great Britain by
Page Bros, Norwich, Norfolk

For Christopher, Anne-Marie, Marcus and Natasha

Contents

Introduction

I still haven't found what I'm looking for. . .

(U2)

There is a feeling generally shared amongst human beings that our lives ought to matter in some way. There must be a reason why we were put onto this earth, or at least, even if there doesn't appear to be one, since we have been given life as a gift, we should attempt to get the most out of it and live it to the full. We are all seeking a life that matters — that matters to ourselves and to other people. If we can achieve in small or large things and leave our mark on the world in our own way then we will have succeeded. This book is an attempt to find a direction in achieving that aim by looking afresh at the 'wisest' book in the Bible — the Book of Proverbs — which is full of good advice about how to lead a successful and meaningful existence. We may well have a desire to better ourselves, morally, religiously or practically. By taking on board the advice of the wise on various issues in life we just might feel that we are able to do that, even in some small area of our lives.

Those who read the Bible make the intriguing discovery that it has fresh insights to offer to each generation. Our own generation is no exception. One part of the Bible, however, remains relatively unexplored, although it speaks profoundly to us in the modern world. This part is known under the collective title of the Wisdom literature, and contains the Books of Proverbs, Job and Ecclesiastes. Their perspective is different from the rest of Holy Scripture in that they begin from human experience of life. God is not absent, but his role is very different from that found elsewhere in the Bible. God created the world and set up the orders to be found in it, but the stress is on the human attempt to understand the world in all its confusing diversity. This way of looking at the world speaks with great relevance to our own generation.

We live in an age in which experience rather than a set of religious beliefs is the starting point for understanding life for most people and in which issues of human relationship with each other and with the world around us are of prime concern. People today are often suspicious of a set of beliefs being presented to them as a 'package' that needs to be taken on trust. This is partly, I think, because there are various 'packages' being presented by different religions and by different parties and groups within those religions. Some might find a set of beliefs which they can happily adopt as their own, but for many individuals there is the feeling that this will compromise their individuality. Many people have what they might term a general moral sense – they do not need to confess faith in the Ten Commandments, for example, to know that killing is wrong. This moral sense is, like the Wisdom literature, grounded in experience, not necessarily in one's own experience but in the experience of the generations, in that which has been passed down in families and social groups, in school perhaps, or as part of one's general education or in religious circles. When calamity strikes there is an attempt to understand but often a desire to give up on God, since faith in God, if it offers no rewards, is seen as a pointless enterprise. Many people, if they have religious faith, believe in a God who created the world, but may find it harder to accept the specifics of, say, Christian belief: that God sent his Son into the world to redeem humankind.

There are, in my view, striking similarities between these

kinds of views and the world view of the Wisdom writers. Centuries may divide us, but human experience has remained much the same since time immemorial. The wise begin from experience, from relationships and from basic observations about how to treat people. They offer advice that is universally true for each generation. There is a profound understanding of human characteristics, the good ones and the bad ones, and of the ease with which standards slip and chaos ensues. There is an appreciation of good things – money, responsibility, marriage, neighbourliness, good friends, good food, carefully spoken words – and warnings against bad things – sloth, deception, quarrelsomeness, lying, foolishness, estrangement. There is interest in family life and values and in society as a whole, betraying a deep pragmatism about the realities of life and yet an interest in upholding an ideal to which people can aspire. There is a healthy mix of viewing life as it is and yet exhorting people to a better and more meaningful life. Wisdom is about helping people to cope with the many choices and decisions they face and about equipping people to react to problems in a mature way. It is about helping people to see things in a fresh light so that they can find untapped resources within themselves that will equip them to cope in times of difficulty. It is about celebrating and giving meaning to the ordinary and everyday experiences that we all, as human beings, share.

In the Book of Proverbs, life is often illuminated by drawing parallels with the created world. Nowadays we have a fresh appreciation of our natural environment and a desire to preserve nature in its diversity, and so the interest of the Wisdom writers in describing nature and creation speaks to us with deep resonance. We have at particular times in our history lost direction in our sense of interaction with our natural environment and so have devalued and abused it. The writers of the Proverbs remind us of the essential relationship that we have with the world around us: they draw our attention to the parallels between animal and human life, they glory at the world through its wonders, and they find God the Creator in the hidden orders that come to light.

For many people in our time, science has replaced superstition in their evaluation of the world. Much of what our ancestors did not understand about the world they categorized in the realm of the mysterious or as the hidden purposes of God. In today's world science has uncovered much of that mystery and the hidden realm becomes smaller, although often one set of answers leads to another set of questions. The method employed by the writers of Proverbs resembles the scientific quest in a number of ways. They are interested in pinning down the chaos around us, in understanding the world, in listing, in ordering, in knowledge. Their mood is one of questioning, of taking nothing for granted, of searching on a universal scale for answers to the mysteries of life. Experience is the great test – maxims are tried and tested by experience, which can be contradictory, but it is in the repetition of experience that truth is eventually found. God is at the limits of this quest for meaning – he is perceived as holding the final answers to everything. He is the Creator who set up the order of nature and set the world in motion. Corresponding to this order is a societal order, a code of moral living that is in harmony with the divine purposes and in this way human behaviour is seen to have an effect on the very structures of the created universe. This is clearly apparent in an age in which, at the press of a button, human ingenuity could blow up the world with a nuclear bomb. The human quest for knowledge can end in chaos – it needs to be directed into the right channels for us all to live satisfying and meaningful lives. The Wisdom literature is aptly named – it takes wisdom to understand life's profundities and contradictions.

Who wrote the Proverbs and when?

Before launching into the meat of the advice that the proverbial material has to offer, we might just ask a few very brief questions about the origins of this material. As we have it today, and as it has been preserved for many thousands of years in the Bible, Proverbs is a collection of sayings. There is little order about them in that the subject matter shifts swiftly from one proverb to another. It appears to be a compendium of accumulated advice rather than a book which has been composed as a whole. It seems clear that an author or a number of authors (or maybe we should call them editors) collected the material and wrote it down at a point in time. Traditionally King Solomon was thought to have written the book (as stated in 1:1 and 10:1), and it may well be that wise men at his court did so. However, there is also a reference within the Book of Proverbs to the 'men of Hezekiah' (25:1, Hezekiah having been a later king of Israel), who are said to have copied proverbs, which suggests that maybe more than one group of 'wise' was responsible for compiling the book. It is quite possible that different sections of the book were penned at different times: Proverbs 1–9 is written in a rather different style from most of the rest of the book and is more overtly religious, leading commentators to deduce that it was written or collected separately from the maxims section in Proverbs 10–31. Even within the maxims section, there are distinct units such as Proverbs 22–24 which has links with an Egyptian instruction and could have been borrowed from that source, and Proverbs 25–9, a section which comes under the 'men of Hezekiah' heading. In addition, in Proverbs 30 and 31 there are separate poems that claim to be the wisdom of particular kings. All these considerations lead to the conclusion that the written history of Proverbs is probably diverse.

The material may also have passed through an oral stage.

Just as in our own culture we have many proverbs that have been verbally passed down within families or communities, so it was in ancient Israel where proverbs were probably of a traditional nature and provided a whole body of ethical advice for both the literate and the illiterate (after all, very few people could read and write in those days).

Another possible source of some of this material is specialist wisdom schools: we know that in Egypt there were such schools for the training of 'the wise' who were an educated elite. However, education may have been more widespread than this and pupils may have clustered around certain elders within a community or certain families who had a scribal or educating role or in local schools with a fairly general curriculum. We do not know for certain what structures existed, but we do know that the courts of kings had their wise counsellors and administrators who also needed to benefit from the fruits of such education. It could be then that we need to deal with these proverbs on different levels – on the one hand they are advice for all and that is how we are treating them, but, on the other, the acquisition of true wisdom and a really sound education is a lifetime activity, and reading, writing and true learning could only be practised by a few. It is the latter category of 'wise men' who might be responsible for the committing of these traditional proverbs to paper. Throughout the book I refer to 'the wise' as a group, meaning those who compiled these proverbs, but we do not know whether they were an identifiable group or whether this was simply a world view perpetuated by the educated. However, it provides a useful term for identifying those who were interested enough to pass on this valuable knowledge.

The Book of Proverbs was certainly written a long time ago. King Solomon reigned in the ninth century BC and King Hezekiah in the seventh, which may mean that much of the book was compiled by the end of the seventh century BC, six centuries before Christ and two thousand years before our own. It is amazing that this ancient wisdom can still speak to us today and guide us in our ethical choices – it is a real witness to the continuity of human nature, human activity and human emotion.

Throughout many decades of scholarly opinion, the Wisdom literature was regarded as the 'poor relation' alongside other, more significant parts of the Hebrew Bible, such as the Law and the Prophets. This was because there is no mention of the great saving events of Israel's history, nor of the great figures such as Moses or David, nor of Israel's special covenant relationship with God. Nor does it contain the usual picture of God as Redeemer of Israel, preferring to focus on God as universal Creator. However, in my opinion, it is these omissions that make it so interesting and so ripe for fresh appreciation today. This literature is of far-reaching significance for our modern age in its concerns with the family, society, and the natural world; it has indeed 'come of age' in our own time. Let us now explore the wisdom of the ancients and see what they have to say to us today. We will focus on the Book of Proverbs as a handbook for making choices in life. The Bible, far from being a modern irrelevance, has some deep insights to reveal, if we only let it speak to us afresh.

1
Retracing the steps of ancient Israelite wisdom

The quest for meaning

> We seal our fates by the choices we make . . .
>
> (Gloria Estefan)

Why is it that we are always wanting to know more, to understand, to learn about and control the world around us? What is it about human nature that leads us to this inquisitiveness about our surroundings? Of course the opening chapters of Genesis tell us that the desire for knowledge is the sin that led to the downfall of humankind. But that desire itself came from somewhere. Is it really plausible that God never intended us to be curious but rather meant us to live in a paradisal world where no questions were asked and no answers were given? There is some truth in the thought that we might gain more inner peace if we stopped looking so frantically for the answers to our unceasing questions. But conversely we find it very satisfying to be able to fulfil our desire for knowledge – it enables us to control our environment, extends the possibilities open to us, even helps us control our own minds and bodies. It is hard to imagine the rate of 'progress' slowing up even if we wanted it to. Of course there are bad aspects to progress, such as our capacity to destroy our planet or despoil our natural habitats, but there are also many benefits, such as our ability to prolong life by medicine and to cure illness, our development of air travel so that we can see much more of the world, and so on.

I suggest that the desire for knowledge, whilst in many ways an end in itself, is none the less bound up with the desire for meaning. We seek to understand hoping that in the end we will have full knowledge and complete control. We seek to be 'like God' (Gen. 3:5, 22) and want to understand the mind of God. Some are confident that one day we will get there and then our quest for understanding will come to an end. Others believe that one question inevitably leads to another and so ultimate knowledge will never be attained. In traditional religious terms such knowledge lies with God and human beings cannot find the way to it – that is certainly the view of the Wisdom writers. Some believe that ultimate knowledge is of a different nature to the kind of knowledge we, as human beings, seek. The tree of the knowledge of good and evil was only one of the trees in the Garden of Eden, alongside the tree of eternal life and presumably others (Gen. 2:16; 3:24). Maybe the quest for knowledge is just one path to God alongside others that we need to consider. Or maybe there is a whole spiritual plane that we, in our quest for knowledge of the material and matter of the universe and its inhabitants, are missing altogether.

Knowledge and meaning are not, however, one and the same. One could presumably lead a meaningful life with no knowledge of much at all. Although certainly a way of giving purpose to our lives, knowledge is just one route to meaning. We need to be busy, to interact with others, to learn and to discover, to make our contribution to the world, however small that may be. Without purpose we wither in a wasteland of boredom. We live in a world where those with purpose are successful and earn salaries that allow them to live well whilst those without purpose drift aimlessly in a sea of poverty, reliant on the charity of those who are able to give a more meaningful structure to their lives. People sometimes mistakenly think of the Garden of Eden as a paradise where one does nothing all day, rather like being on holiday all the time and basking in the sun. But in fact Adam was given the job of tending the garden (Gen. 2:15) – a little light gardening gave him a purpose in that paradisal existence alongside his enjoyment of his relationship with Eve and of their relationship with God. We know that even on holiday, if we were to lie in the sun and do nothing but sleep we would soon be bored – we need our blockbuster novel, or our Walkman, or a few postcards to write at the very least!

The Wisdom writers, presenting common human experience accumulated over many centuries, realized that work was an essential ingredient of life and chastised those who were too lazy to bother. They saw wealth as the corollary of a successful working life and poverty as the inevitable result of the laziness trap. Human beings learned early on that they needed to do something with their lives; they needed purpose, they needed work and they wanted to know more. So arose the attempt to classify the world around them by the use of proverbs, likening human behaviour to natural phenomena or to other, un-related, aspects of human life or classifying unrelated things by numbering them or riddling and questioning to make people sit up and think. These were their methods of expressing the quest for meaning.

In the maxims the wise developed a whole compendium of advice based on observation of human behaviour. One common theme is their experience that simple, uncompli-cated lives and attitudes were better than complex ones. It was easier not to have too many goods and chattels because then you didn't have to worry that they might be stolen. It was easier – and also wiser – to hold your tongue than to be considered a foolish babbler. They did not advocate a monkish renunciation of the world – far from it. They advised living life to the full and enjoying all the pleasures of the world but in moderation and with a healthy cynicism and a strong dose of common sense that would help men and women to steer a meaningful path through the many distractions waiting to grab their attention. Wisdom then is good common sense, based on experience, which has as its aim the desire to make life as meaningful and uncomplicated as possible.

Of course, it is easy to classify the world and put things into neat pigeonholes, but we all know that from time to time disastrous things occur that threaten to upset the neat ordered life we create for ourselves. The wise men of Proverbs were aware of life's contradictions, but did not deal on a profound level with problems of suffering beyond what was comprehensible within the system. That was left to the author of Job who provides us with the test case of someone who leads a good life of the kind the Wisdom writers advocated but is nevertheless afflicted by disasters that leave him wondering what the basis of his relationship with God really was. Brought almost to the brink of losing his faith, for Job it is not the quest for knowledge that provides the answer he is looking for, but rather the realization that God's knowledge far surpasses that of human beings. Here we come up against the idea of the limits of knowledge, something of which the writers of Proverbs were also distinctly aware.

Whether we believe in God and the possibility of a relationship with him or not, most of us would acknowledge that there is a spiritual dimension to life. Many people today find that they are able to tune into the more spiritual side of their nature by listening to music or by making use of contemplation techniques. Some look to other people and helping others to give their life meaning – although sometimes people inevitably let each other down. Others look for inspiration in beautiful landscapes, or foreign travel, or luxurious houses and many possessions. There are many things in life that afford meaning to us as well as our own generation of meaning by our personal efforts. There is a two-way interplay between our own strivings to give shape to our lives, to find partners, to have children, to build happy homes, to find interesting work, and our reliance on external things to give us a sense of well-being such as music, art, fiction and drama or sport and physical exercise – hatever interests us or stimulates our senses.

The further question is whether these aspects of our human existence remain fully satisfying for us or whether we need a more clearly divine dimension to our lives. Do we have room for God in our busy lives? Do we really need him? Should we make time for him or is he a superfluous aspect of our existence? The wise men were apparently more interested in human concerns than divine ones. They saw God as being on the sidelines, the source of ultimate meaning but not part of the day-to-day work of understanding and controlling the world. Many people today treat God in the same way – he is there for the bad times, for times of grief and loneliness or for times of ceremony and commitment, but on a day-to-day level he is edged out – after all we wouldn't want to be seen as a religious freak. There is a fear of what others might think if we suddenly 'became religious'. We live in a world, at least in the West, where the secular rather than the religious is often normality. For the wise this was almost the case too – certainly they lived in a more overtly religious world than we do today but within that world they managed to be the least religious of the lot! Their belief in God was in a Creator who set the world up, but not in one who intervened in human life on a day-to-day level. Many people today also believe in this kind of God who created the world but then left it to run of its own accord. Suffering is comprehensible within this framework – it is not God's fault but the fault of humans treating each other badly. Even natural disasters are not evil intentions on the part of God but intrinsic to the order that God set in motion. This is in many ways where the Wisdom writers are coming from. They are more interested in getting on with life than musing on the divine or worrying about divine intervention in miracles or disasters. They want to find an order that can be relied upon and to work life out according to that order. This is why the Wisdom literature rings many chords with modern attitudes and why we might be interested to learn more about it.

Life as a path

It is often only with hindsight that we are able to look back over a series of events that have happened in our lives and find some pattern in them. We think perhaps of fortuitous events that have influenced our lives in a massive way, such as meeting a lifelong partner or an opening in our chosen career that then led on to many other opportunities. We can also recall bad things that seemed senseless at the time but sometimes, with hindsight, had further more positive repercussions. Examples might be the senseless death of a loved one or a piece of bad luck in business. It is human nature to look for patterns in life: while some believe that there is an overall pattern operational in our lives, others put it all down to pure chance. In Guy Gavriel Kay's fantasy novel *The Fionavar Tapestry,* the actions of human beings over several generations help to create a large tapestry which gradually makes up a picture that will one day be complete. The human beings are not controlled in what they do – they can put the needle and thread back into the tapestry at whichever point they wish. However, the question is posed, how does the needle come back to the front again? That is seen to be the realm of God so that the tapestry is the product of a delicate interchange between opportunities offered by God and actions carried out by human beings. This is a helpful way of understanding patterns in life. We do have control over our actions and are free to act in whatever way seems right at the time, but there are times when we get the feeling that life is not entirely random and that we are being given a helping hand. And that helping hand may not necessarily be a good one: it could just as well be a hindrance, at least at first sight.

In their quest for patterns the wise men liked the image of life as a path. By working out what wise behaviour consisted of, human beings could map out their lives. They knew that if they gossiped, for example, there were potentially harmful results. They could end up being accused of speaking out of turn, or they could lose friends through the experience and gain enemies. So, they concluded, it was best simply not to do it. Then they knew that in that area of their life at least they would be free from problems. By applying such dictums to all areas of life, a foolproof system could be devised that meant a happy, successful, stress-free life. Of course we all know that unexpected things come up – one cannot plan one's life in quite such a neat way. We are all subject to chance. We do not know whom we will meet, what doors will open or close, who will influence us, or what adventures and experiences we will have. But we can be fairly sure that if we have a set of values that we can follow, we will at least be equipped to face any challenges that come to meet us. If we are wise – people of integrity – others will recognize it and will have the confidence to trust us and rely on us so that in the end we will become those with influence and power in our own generation.

Another aspect of the image of life as a path is that it is not static. Rather, as we make progress along the path we come nearer to our goal and we grow in understanding along the way. There have been many stories about adventurers setting out on a path – one thinks perhaps of Frodo Baggins in Tolkien's *The Lord of the Rings*. Having set out, there is no turning back, and if and when the adventurer returns home at the end of the journey, as Baggins does, things cannot and will not ever be the same again. The externals may have remained the same, but the person is fundamentally changed by the experience that he or she has undergone, by the people encountered and by the challenges that have been faced and overcome. Life is rather like this. It is a constant learning process and once we have learnt a skill, or overcome a fear, or become used to a certain way of doing things, they are no longer fresh challenges but become normality. Some people reach a point where they feel that they have enough responsibility and they have faced enough challenges, and they are happy to stay still for a while. Others go on wanting more and more, never satisfied, always wanting to push themselves further. One might liken this to downhill paths and uphill ones. There is an upward gradient at the beginning of one's life but then some choose to level out sooner than others and then go downhill gradually. Others go up a steeper gradient and yet the ultimate fall is often quicker and more dramatic. Any path is legitimate – each is a learning and growing experience for the individual and all our paths intersect with each other from time to time.

As we move along life's path our perceptions and desires change; we inevitably reach different stages in life and our wishes and dreams change. Along that path we are faced with decisions that affect our future and, of course, we are just as likely to make a wrong decision and start going in the wrong direction as in the right one. Curiously enough, however, we soon know when we have taken a false turn. This is not to say that many different routes may be right for us, but we tend to know fairly quickly when a chosen job or a chosen partner is wrong for us and then there is a difficult process of disentanglement and of reconciliation with ourselves before we get back on the main path again. In the words of the well-known song by Gloria Estefan, we indeed seal our fates by the choices we make – some decisions are more irreversible than others and we all have to deal with regrets in life, things we have left undone or things we ought not to have done.

The Wisdom writers were very much aware of choices and saw the path of wisdom as a series of good choices and sound decisions: 'So you will walk in the way of good men and keep to the paths of the righteous' (Prov. 2:20). This was the path to life, happiness and well-being as well as to longevity and many blessings. It was characterized as a smooth, straight path, in modern terms rather like a well-built, concrete road. The other option was the path that led to death, the seemingly alluring but wrong choices, such as spending time with prostitutes or partaking in foolish gossip or in unfair dealings with people. This was the way of evil, associating with those 'who forsake the paths of uprightness to walk in the ways of darkness, who rejoice in doing evil and delight in the perverseness of evil; men whose paths are crooked, and who are devious in their ways' (Prov. 2:13–15). This in turn was characterized as a path full of ruts and holes, twisting and turning, with all sorts of unexpected obstacles, like a winding and muddy woodland path surrounded by trees and covered by roots. The path of wisdom and its benefits in Proverbs 1 is closely followed by a description of sinners and the enticements which allure them:

> My son, do not walk in the way with them,
>   hold back your foot from their paths;
> for their feet run to evil,
>   and they make haste to shed blood.
> For in vain is a net spread in the sight of any
>   bird;
> but these men lie in wait for their own
>   blood,
>   they set an ambush for their own lives.

> Such are the ways of all who get gain by
>   violence;
>   it takes away the life of its possessors.
>   (Prov. 1:15–19)

Those who perpetuate violence want to get others on their side. Although they set traps for their unsuspecting victims, the only traps they are really setting, say the wise, are for themselves as they slide deeper and deeper into sin. This is why it is important to receive the kind of instruction that the wise offer in order to combat these temptations. There are warnings, therefore, against straying from the right path. It is easy to stray from paths and get lost, deliberately or not, and so we read the rather bald statement that 'A man who wanders from the way of understanding will rest in the assembly of the dead' (Prov. 21:16; cf. Prov. 14:12; 16:25). This may refer to premature death which is often considered the end of the path of folly, or it may be saying that the fool is as good as dead because his lack of wisdom deprives him of true 'life'. Life is seen as a journey on which we face many choices, the ultimate one of which is the choice between the increase of life or the path towards death, succinctly expressed in Proverbs 12:28: 'In the path of righteousness is life, but the way of error leads to death.'

The wise had a rather black and white view of the world: life was either a series of good decisions or a series of bad ones. Of course we know that generally our lives are made up of both good and bad decisions – there is rather more of a mixture than this picture of the two paths suggests. However, on the other hand, it is often true that once on the slippery slope downhill, one evil deed leads to another. The tragic stories of the novelist Thomas Hardy all contain one initial fatal event that leads the hero on to a series of other mistakes that eventuate in self-destruction. In *The Mayor of Casterbridge* that fatal event is the wife-selling that opens the book. Bad choices can lead to bad consequences, which in turn lead us to deprecate ourselves, lose control of our direction and purpose and make more bad choices. However, this chain can be halted, and we – sometimes with the help of others – can lift ourselves out of the holes we dig for ourselves.

Wisdom is seen as available to all. Everyone is able to make good decisions, to behave in appropriate ways and live in harmony with others if they want to. The wise are concerned that each person should be responsible for themselves, an attitude which resonates very much with our own age's 'look after number one' mentality. However, they go a step further. In addition, they advocate good treatment of others and a looking outside of ourselves to consider the effect we are having on others, which we would do well to remember. Although there is some truth in the survival of the fittest idea – that if you don't get there first someone else will – all too often the 'number one' mentality leads us to run roughshod over others. We certainly cannot afford to be left behind, but, warn the wise, do things in the proper way; learn appropriate behaviour and then good things will inevitably come your way.

The wise make the distinction that is often made in religious circles between the righteous and the wicked. They also make other distinctions: between the wise man and the fool, between the rich and the poor, and between the diligent person and the sluggard, or lazy bones. Here, too, in real life such distinctions are often blurred. The righteous/wicked distinction is particularly difficult to maintain: how can we judge another according to such criteria? The only person we are really in a position to judge is ourselves. We may admire others as role models, which they may well be, but ultimately we cannot and should not pontificate about their righteousness or otherwise. The word 'righteousness' in itself needs some unpacking: it is presented as an absolute quality which, in its ideal form, presumably no one can attain except God. It is best to regard it as an ideal for which we strive. In the same way pure wickedness is not likely to be a category into which any one person falls: rather it is a statement about the potential cumulative effect of many evil deeds and attitudes. With any luck adopting the right kind of wise attitudes will lead to righteousness. But what happens when the righteous person finds all kinds of calamities coming his or her way, like Job? Can a righteous person retain personal faith when enduring hardships or illness or loss of family or reputation, and so on?

It is in the face of misfortune that many people's faith crumbles. They had expected religion to be about living a good life and being rewarded for it in just the way that the wise seem to advocate. How can we make sense of our lives in the face of the unforeseen calamities that do sometimes occur? Well, I suppose not even the wise thought that unlimited happiness was our apportioned lot. Life is full of 'ups' and 'downs' and if there were no 'downs' we would not know what 'ups' are. The good things of life tend to be even better in the light of the bad. I am not advocating suffering as a necessary corollary to good, but often, through suffering, good can come and the person who has both suffered and prospered will often appreciate prosperity more for having had those previous experiences. The complex tapestry of life is not one-dimensional – it has many faces and aspects. We are advised to do all we can to lead a life that takes us on the path of wisdom but there may be an uneven road ahead that will temporarily knock us off course. We must not let these bumps and thorns lead us off the road completely. Rather we should strive to re-gain our steady road and learn from the experiences that we face along the way. This advice is as relevant today as it was to people thousands of years ago who listened to the wisdom of the sages.

The wonders of the natural world

There is an increasing awareness in our age of the need to protect and conserve the world around us. But that has not always been the case. The Judaeo-Christian religion has often been blamed for promulgating the idea that human beings have dominion (Gen. 1:26) and therefore can exploit the planet for their own uses. This is not in fact what dominion means: in stark contrast to mastery and exploitation, it is rather a call to responsible leadership and careful management. However, all too often it has not been interpreted in that way. In the name of progress, we have lost that essential unity with nature that our ancestors enjoyed. Many of us live in towns and cities and rarely have time to appreciate the countryside. Many of us have pets but we are unaware of the animal world at large. In our bid to advance we disturb whole ecosystems, destroying trees and landscapes. We build motorways for our cars and ever increasing numbers of buildings for our growing population without thought for the habitats that we are destroying along the way and for the pollution we are causing. We thus neglect to live in harmony with animals, plants, birds, fish and all aspects of nature around us.

We are beginning to realize afresh in today's world our essential need for an appreciation of the created world. We are learning the harmful effects of trying unnaturally to control animals for food or plants for cultivation. We are aware of the potentially frightening consequences of scientific developments such as cloning and unnatural production of animals and food for human consumption, which need to be monitored. Rather than the presupposition that the natural world is simply there to be harnessed for human control, we need to adopt the attitude of the sages – that of wonder at the world around us, of essential interaction with it grounded in a deep sense of respect. The Wisdom writers discerned a God-ordained order in which everything has a place. They believed that these patterns and structures are there for a purpose, and that, when we exploit and subdue, we are upsetting the natural order.

As the wise looked at the world around them they drew from it similes, metaphors, images and comparisons. They had a close relationship with plants and animals and saw themselves as in essential relationship with the natural world, just as God was too. They observed animal behaviour and drew from it metaphors for human behaviour, as for example, 'Let a man meet a she-bear robbed of her cubs rather than a fool in his folly' (Prov. 17:12). Sometimes they used animal imagery to make amusing parallels such as Proverbs 26:11 and 17: 'Like a dog that returns to his vomit is a fool that repeats his folly' and 'He who meddles in a quarrel not his own is like one who takes a passing dog by the ears.' The first is a lesson in not repeating your mistakes and the second in not interfering in other people's business!

They marvelled at the natural world, rather than claiming to understand it, and sought to articulate their wonder by listing and numbering, rather like our modern 'riddle me ree' rhymes ('My first is in x, my second in y'). One such rhyme is:

> Three things are too wonderful for me;
>   four I do not understand:
> the way of an eagle in the sky,
>   the way of a serpent on a rock,
> the way of a ship on the high seas,
>   and the way of a man with a maiden.
>   (Prov. 30:18–19)

Here four quite natural but diverse features of life have been brought together under the catchword 'way' in a clever align-ment by someone who obviously loved to play with words.

The wise looked at the ways of insects and animals and likened them to the path of wisdom:

> Four things on earth are small,
>> but they are exceedingly wise:
> the ants are a people not strong,
>> yet they provide their food in the
>>> summer;
> the badgers are a people not mighty,
>> yet they make their homes in the rocks;
> the locusts have no king,
>> yet all of them march in rank;
> the lizard you can take in your hands,
>> yet it is in kings' palaces.
>> (Prov. 30:24–9)

They also looked at large, stately animals and compared them to the king:

> Three things are stately in their tread;
>> four are stately in their stride:
> the lion, which is mightiest among beasts
>> and does not turn back before any;
> the strutting cock, the he-goat,
>> and a king striding before his people.
>> (Prov. 30:29–31)

And so the Wisdom writers can recapture for us some of what we have lost concerning our interrelationship with nature. The beauty of the created world can lead us to humility. At once gentle and harsh, the natural world has a value in and of itself without the need for humans to value it since it is all part of God's world that he has created.

The Judaeo-Christian tradition, unlike many nature and fertility religions, has never held that the natural world is divine. The advantage of those religions is that a respect for nature is engendered by the divinity accorded to it. The disadvantage is that inanimate objects and sometimes animals are worshipped as gods, placing them above their natural status and diminishing worship of God. The relationship which the Wisdom literature espouses is one of equality and difference, of a healthy respect and a mutual assistance between human and animal. The wise taught good treatment of animals: 'A righteous man has regard for the life of his beast' (Prov. 12:10). They believed in using animals for human benefit but without exploiting them mercilessly.

The quest for understanding

The ultimate point of trying to comprehend human relationships and patterns in behaviour, which can then be related to God and the world, is the quest for understanding. When you know how to live your life, how to tune in to the order of the universe, how to fulfil God's purposes, then you have true understanding. There are other qualities that accompany such understanding and Proverbs 1 states that the purpose of this collection of proverbs is:

> That men may know wisdom and
>   instruction,
>   understand words of insight,
> receive instruction in wise dealing,
>   righteousness, justice, and equity;
> that prudence may be given to the simple,
>   knowledge and discretion to the youth –
> the wise man also may hear and increase in
>   learning
>   and the man of understanding acquire
>   skill,

to understand a proverb and a figure,
  the words of the wise and their riddles.
                                            (Prov. 1:2–6)

Here, while alongside wisdom understanding is at the top
of the agenda and, according to the precepts of the wise,
the ultimate goal in order to lead a fulfilled life, it is clear
that its by-products are insight, skill, justice, righteousness
and equity. This is the conclusion that might well be drawn
from many of the proverbs on different topics that we
shall be considering, but there are also some proverbs that
specifically treat understanding as a concept.

Much of the language of the Wisdom writers speaks of
looking at something in order to take it in. When we look
away from someone or something, it is a sign that we are
not fully concentrating. When we look at someone or
something intently and with interest, we give our full con-
centration. And so we read that 'A man of understanding
sets his face toward wisdom, but the eyes of a fool are on
the ends of the earth' (Prov. 17:24). The fool is not just
looking away: he is looking beyond and dreaming for the
stars. Foolish daydreaming will get you nowhere, but practical action, say the wise, is the key to success. The fool is
the opposite of the wise man in these proverbs: the percep-
tive person keeps wisdom in sight and concentrates on the
task in hand, but the fool's attention wanders and he learns
nothing. The fool is more wrapped up in himself than in
anyone else: 'A fool takes no pleasure in understanding, but
only in expressing his opinion' (Prov. 18:2). We have all
met people who enjoy talking about themselves too much
and seem oblivious to this fact. Although we realize it
sometimes stems from insecurity and we can be understanding about it, nevertheless it does not facilitate two-
way communication. Such people are often smug and self-
centred; they are in love with their own ideas and cannot
take on board and weigh up the opinions of others; they are

unteachable and yet constantly betray their lack of real understanding and, because they often don't think before they speak, they dig themselves into difficult holes. On the other hand, some self-esteem is important. We should not take a back seat in life and let others take the lead, nor should we lose ourselves in self-hatred. There is a balance to be found.

On the positive side of the coin we read, 'He who gets wisdom loves himself; he who keeps understanding will prosper' (Prov. 19:8). Here the man of understanding is virtually synonymous with the wise man. The wise person must have a sense of self-esteem, even of self-love, for there are many problems that stem from self-hatred such as insecurity or a dislike of one's own company and consequent dependence upon others. Wisdom enhances one's own vitality and therefore does oneself a good turn as well as other people. Understanding is a firm foundation for life, 'By wisdom a house is built, and by understanding it is established; by knowledge the rooms are filled with all precious and pleasant riches' (Prov. 24:3–4). Wisdom not only leads to material prosperity but it establishes sure foundations that ensure domestic well-being and a good life. Right principles lead to all good things. Knowledge then, while not an end in itself, is an essential key to understanding and to wisdom. All these qualities combine together.

Foundational values from Proverbs 1–9

Before considering the maxims in more detail in later chapters we will start by looking at the first nine chapters of Proverbs which reflect on the benefits that wisdom can bring. It is in this section that we find the idea of the two paths most fully expressed. We also discover that wisdom is a two-way process: knowledge, insight and understanding are qualities a person strives to acquire but ultimately they belong to God and are given by him. This does not mean that human beings cannot develop their own gifts, but that all gifts reflect the divine: they are attributes of God and so the lines of communication run in two directions: 'For the Lord gives wisdom; from his mouth come knowledge and understanding; he stores up sound wisdom for the upright; he is a shield to those who walk in integrity, guarding the paths of justice and preserving the way of his saints' (Prov. 2:6–8). Having established this principle, Proverbs 1–9 then puts good and bad behaviour, and the consequences of each, firmly into the framework of faith in God. It is like tuning into a radio station: at first the reception and sound may be poor and it is not until we finely tune the knob that we get clarity. The relationship between human wisdom and God's wisdom works in the same way.

An important part of allowing this two-way traffic to become operational is to do all we can to follow human wisdom while ultimately trusting in God's wisdom: 'Trust in the Lord with all your heart, and do not rely on your own insight. In all your ways acknowledge him, and he will make straight your paths' (Prov. 3:5–6). Human insight can get us a long way, but sometimes events occur that are incomprehensible or we find ourselves at the limits of our understanding. It is at this point that God is to be found and he can be trusted since he represents those higher qualities for which we have been striving. Ultimately it is the fear of God which is true wisdom, as we read in Proverbs 1:7, 2:5–6, and then many more times throughout the book. This is a recognition that God holds the key to all wisdom and so to fear him is to embrace his wisdom which supersedes anything that human beings may attain. Human wisdom, although it reflects divine wisdom, will only ever be a poor copy.

So, Proverbs 1–9 addresses foundational issues such as the nature of wisdom and the acquisition of knowledge and understanding. It also introduces the allegories of Woman Wisdom and Woman Folly, who are strongly contrasted. In Proverbs 1:20 the figure of Woman Wisdom is portrayed as standing on the street corner calling to passers-by to join the wisdom team, rather like a town crier or a politician on a soap-box: 'Wisdom cries aloud in the street; in the markets she raises her voice.' In chapter 9 Wisdom is pictured calling loudly through her messengers whom she has sent out to invite whoever desires wisdom to come to a meal she has prepared. She calls for the young to put aside their immaturity and to walk in her ways. Wisdom is a precious gift, part of the essence of the universe.

We read in Proverbs 3:19 that 'The Lord by wisdom founded the earth; by understanding he established the heavens.' It is later in Proverbs 8, however, that a full description of Woman Wisdom is found. Although herself created by God, she was present and taking delight in the world as it was created. She thus stands at the heart of the order that is the pattern placed upon the world at creation. To live in harmony with wisdom, then, is to live in harmony with the whole of God's creation. The reader is enjoined to love her and seek her.

It is perhaps surprising to read that Woman Wisdom participated in creation itself. She is seen as a kind of channel between God, the Creator and Orderer, and humanity who can strive to understand such wonders by acquiring wisdom. It is interesting to note that an essential part of God's creative activity is described in terms of the feminine. We are far more used to masculine portrayals of God as Father, for example, than feminine ones. It was through feminine Wisdom that creation was effected and she was the first to delight in the world which God made.

Her antithesis is Woman Folly who is portrayed as an adulteress using her charm and powers of argument to persuade. She has been unfaithful to her husband and has no moral affiliation. The fullest description of Woman Folly is found in Proverbs 5 where the extent of her seductive nature is made clear. Her lips drip honey and her speech is oily, but ultimately her path leads to death. The uneducated are told to keep away and to be faithful only to wisdom. In Proverbs 7 the injunctions to keep the commandments and avoid loose females are reiterated. It is interesting that Woman Folly also speaks of love, but it is a sexual love which will only last through the night.

A great deal of emphasis is placed in chapters 1 and 2 on the need to acquire wisdom – it doesn't just happen. It is very true that anything we learn from scratch takes a great deal of effort on our part – and it doesn't get any easier as we get older! It is equally true that acquiring wisdom requires a great deal of listening and effort on our part as we strive to understand these difficult concepts. True wisdom belongs to God but people can tune into his wisdom if they make the effort to acquire it. One of the main reasons to do so is to avoid the path of folly, which is an easy, false path requiring no education.

We are told in Proverbs 3 that longevity is one of the gifts of wisdom, and that loyalty and faithfulness are her keywords. Trust in God is another key. There is a danger today, as also in the past, of human beings being over-confident about their own potential. Sometimes we need to realize all that we do not know and do not fully under-stand. So, Proverbs 3:7–8 tells us: 'Be not wise in your own eyes; fear the Lord, and turn away from evil. It will be healing to your flesh and refreshment to your bones.' It is interesting that trusting in God is said to give relief to the body. It is certainly very true that when we just sit back and let someone else do things for us it is very relaxing. Sitting back and letting God take control of our lives has the same effect.

Proverbs 3 makes mention of harvest offerings. It tells us that by giving to God the first fruits of the harvest as an act of thanks we secure future blessing. But although God wonderfully provides, he also chastises and so we must expect discipline from God in the same way that a father disciplines his child.

Wisdom depends on good behaviour and, at the end of chapter 3, we begin to find proverbs that are similar in style to those in Proverbs 10–31. We read, for example, 'Do not withhold good from those to whom it is due, when it is in your power to do it' (Prov. 3:27). We are all called to help each other where we can. We are also warned in Proverbs 3 against playing silly power games with people, such as our neighbours, and are told not to quarrel without good reason (v. 30). Another trap which we are told to avoid is envy of those who may be attractive in various ways, whether it be for their actions or their wealth or their deeds. If they are on the path of wickedness, the warning is to keep away!

These chapters then give us an introduction to many of the themes that we will be considering later in this book, such as wealth, relationships, handling anger, and so on. In chapter 6, for example, there are warnings against making pledges or loans of money, which may lead into the trap of indebtedness or even to ending up under the thumb of another. How many of us have felt the 'trap' of a mortgage or loan? This feeling is made worse if it is a friend or neighbour who has lent us money, as it destroys the sense of equality between us as well as our own personal freedom. We will return to the topic of money again later in the book. There are also proverbs on laziness, alerting the listener to the fact that too much sleep can cause a person to slip into poverty (Prov. 6:10–11).

The keeping of commandments is recommended by the wise rather than going down the path of adultery. There is a particular warning against sleeping with a neighbour's wife, a sin which will lead to harsh punishment. Thieves too will be severely punished, as will adulterers when the husband finds out what has been happening with his wife. Young men are also advised to avoid foolish women too, those who entice but whose promises are empty and worthless.

There are warnings against crooked speech introducing the theme of communication which was very important to the wise, as we shall see. Being ensnared by the clever talk of others is a trap of which one must certainly beware. In Proverbs 9 scoffers are mentioned, a reminder to the modern reader perhaps of schoolchildren who scoff at the bright child in the class, largely because they themselves cannot aspire to such achievement. Scoffing is a sign of immaturity which is practised by the wicked. It is a well-known feature of adolescence – it is much easier to mock than to succeed. Scoffers hate being told off, but that is what the wise person must be prepared to accept.

Proverbs 1–9 then is about the choices and pitfalls that await unsuspecting youths embarking upon life. They are about making an active decision to choose wisdom and to choose God, rather than folly and death. You would think that the choice was easy, but there seems to be a recognition on the part of the wise that for human beings it is natural to err and that the straight path is not such a simple choice. The way of wisdom is the way of God, which is why the religious issues being addressed in this section are foundational. Wisdom brings blessing to those who are willing to receive and study it, as the opening section of chapter 4 makes clear: 'Prize her highly, and she will exalt you; she will honour you if you embrace her' (v. 8). The path of wisdom contrasts with the path of evil. Those who listen hard will hear wisdom's voice and will lay aside all crooked speech. By focusing on the path ahead the wise will avoid the temptation to look around the corner at the paths of the wicked.

This first section of Proverbs is often thought to have been borne of more serious theological reflection, and perhaps to have been written after the main body of sayings, drawing wider conclusions in the light of the accumulation of pieces of individual advice. We find mention, for example, of the deeper emotion of love, which is lacking in the main collection of sayings, and in particular love in relationship to God. We read in Proverbs 3:12, 'The Lord reproves him whom he loves', which also indicates the importance in the eyes of the wise of disciplining those you love. This is a sentiment echoed in Proverbs 9:8 in relation to people's dealings with one with another, 'reprove a wise man and he will love you', which speaks of the importance of honest words, even if they are not very palatable! In Proverbs 3:3 there is also the idea of covenant loyalty or steadfast love: 'Let not loyalty and faithfulness forsake you; bind them about your heart. Then you will win favour and a good name in the sight of God and man.' There is also the exhortation to love Wisdom in Proverbs 4:6: 'Love her and she will guard you.'

What, then, are the benefits of wisdom? Why should we take this advice to heart? Wisdom offers us an understanding of many things – of righteousness as well as of justice and of equity. It advocates the qualities of prudence and discretion which can be learned through the deep understanding of human nature offered by the proverbs. It promotes knowledge and learning, and the acquisition of skill of all types, not just cleverness in the formulation of riddles or proverbs or clever words but any skill, however humble. It is, say the wise, the motivation and inner heart of the person that is important, not their status or innate ability. But wisdom is not a *fait accompli*, for we can all strive to better ourselves, however good we might think we are already. Even the stupid can gain understanding and develop abilities as long as they are willing to put in the effort required in order to acquire the skill. The wise do not have time for people who say that they cannot do things and cannot succeed. They congratulate those who are willing to try. There is a strong feeling in the Wisdom writings of making the most of oneself, of stretching oneself

to the maximum, of making something of oneself in whatever way possible. They call us to look at our whole selves,
at the whole picture of our lives, at our morality and our
relationship with God. How can we improve our emotional
and practical lives so that we more properly resemble the
person we want to be rather than the person we are? There
have always been wise and there have always been foolish,
say the Wisdom writers – which will you choose to be?

2

Maxims about personal and emotive concerns in life

Work

> I work all night, I work all day
> to pay the bills I have to pay . . . (Abba)

Many people would feel a lack of direction and lack of objective in their lives if they did not work. We traditionally think of work as paid employment, but in the sense of the proverbial literature it means any kind of constructive and productive activity. Work gives a structure to a day and it brings us into contact with others: there is nothing more rewarding than a job done well. Some people are able to combine their hobbies and their work, while others, who may be unable to work through illness or disability, may still be able to find reward in certain activities that they are able to undertake. The key is the desire to do something fulfilling with one's life rather than to give in to laziness and self-indulgence. It is assumed throughout the proverbs that all men (and it was men in those days who worked in any formal sense), whatever their station in life, would work. We don't find the concept of the idle rich here – even the king had a job to do.

The sages also recognized the practical side of working – the need to pay the bills. Many proverbs involve a contrast, and in this context the dangers of laziness are contrasted with the benefits of work: 'A slack hand causes poverty, but the hand of the diligent makes rich' (Prov. 10:4). 'A slack hand' refers to a half-hearted effort by a person, which in those days could pose the real threat of actual destitution. The opposite is hard work which leads to prosperity: not riches in the sense of excessive wealth but sufficient income to ensure economic security. This is what most of us strive for – an economic security that will mean that we don't have to worry about money especially in our retirement and old age. We also read in similar vein: 'He who tills his land will have plenty of bread, but he who follows worthless pursuits has no sense' (Prov. 12:11). Work is seen to be a useful and worthwhile activity in contrast to 'worthless pursuits'. In this reference to tilling the land, indicating serious farming, we find an agricultural theme that runs through many of the proverbs. Farming is considered a worthwhile activity, and working the soil is often contrasted with the activities of the dilettante who wastes time and fritters away his energies. Such a person is considered to be deficient in good sense. Careful, steady work is better than chasing rainbows. We might have expected here that the result of following worthless pursuits would be a lack of bread, in strict parallelism with the first half of the proverb (cf. the close parallel of Proverbs 28:19 which does give the expected result: 'He who tills his land will have plenty of bread, but he who follows worthless pursuits will have plenty of poverty'), but instead in Proverbs 12:11 we are simply told of the quality of mind of the one involved in such pursuits. Presumably the inference here is that some occupations are more worthwhile than others. 'Worthless pursuits' may refer to purposeless, unsteady, possibly immoral, occupations rather than complete idleness.

The slothful/diligent comparison is a popular one amongst the wise. We read, 'A slothful man will not catch his prey, but the diligent man will get precious wealth' (Prov. 12:27). The implication in this metaphor from hunting is that the idle person is too lazy to provide food for himself and his family. He lacks the energy and sense of urgency needed to bring an enterprise to a successful conclusion. On the other hand the diligent person will attain precious possessions, themselves the outcome of hard work carried out to make provision for himself and his family. Thus, the work ethic leading to prosperity is alive and well in the proverbs. Diligence in work is the key. It is no good doing a scrappy, hurried job: the worker needs to take real pride in his work. It is interesting that in all of the proverbs I have mentioned so far, the theme of food is closely linked with the work/laziness theme.

Work leads to success and to power: 'The hand of the diligent will rule, while the slothful will be put to forced labour' (Prov. 12:24). Here, two extremes – ruling the country and working in a labour camp – are used as vivid illustrations. This raises the issue of autonomy. While the diligent person becomes master of his own fate and is no longer dependent on anyone else, the lazy person could find himself in a position of slavery, or certainly in a job in which he is forced to labour. It is ironic that those who like work and so rise to the top find themselves in a position where they no longer have to engage in it, whilst those who hate work end up labouring!

Work gives a person responsibility over others and the context in which to develop the ability to manage them. It employs the mind and fosters skills. It is a large part of a person's identity and gives shape and meaning to life. 'The soul of the sluggard craves, and gets nothing, while the soul of the diligent is richly supplied' (Prov. 13:4). The word 'soul' here refers to desire. The lazy live frustrated lives because they desire many things but their appetites remain unsatisfied because they are not prepared to put in the hard work required to achieve their aims. The desires of those who work hard are on the other hand easily satisfied – they are made fat and prosperous. This proverb provides the interesting insight that while lazy people are always wanting more without putting in the effort involved to get it, all successful people have had to work hard at some time in their lives, even if later on they can rest and enjoy the fruits of their toil. Respect is not earned for nothing and making a name for oneself involves sheer dedication on a profound level. The wise attempt to stir the lazy into action before it is too late. Laziness is a barren land that leads nowhere, whilst industriousness is an honest engagement with the real world.

And the wise did not like idle chatter either: 'In all toil there is profit, but mere talk tends only to want' (Prov. 14:23). We hear too much talk today of doing the minimum to get by and to ensure that the pay packet arrives at the end of the week. This proverb is saying that there is no point talking about it, get on and work at it, whatever your goal may be! Physical labour is better than worthless chatter and idle boasting; deeds are better than words. Again, as with laziness, verbosity is a barren occupation which produces nothing but want, whereas solid work leads to real gain.

The wise are not only disparaging of those who are lazy but of those who do not work hard. They maintain: 'He who is slack in his work is a brother to him who destroys' (Prov. 18:9). This time without the use of contrast, the proverb likens the person who is slack in work to someone who is deliberately destructive – there is little difference since the slothful person ruins things just as effectively as a person who has set out to destroy. 'Brother' here refers to one of a similar nature rather than to a relative. Failure to work with care and commitment then is judged in an equivalent manner to setting out deliberately to destroy. For example, it makes little difference if a car will not work properly because it has been poorly made by indolent employees of a car firm, or because it has been deliberately ransacked – the car that was perfect on the production line is soon rendered useless if it is deliberately tampered with. In both scenarios the result is exactly the same – the car does not work. The fact that the car was improperly made is actually worse because the employees, who should have had the conscientiousness to want to do a good day's work and produce worthwhile goods, have failed in their obligation, whereas the wrecker has rather less commitment in the first place.

Slackness is seen to unleash all kinds of negative emotions. There is nothing more soul-destroying than to have too little work and not feel stretched, or to feel bored and unmotivated, or to have to try and extend a short task to take as long as possible. Deliberate slackness over a long period of time makes us slow and surly, unmotivated and uninteresting to others. It can quickly lead on to further negativity and destructiveness both towards ourselves and towards other people, as the wise recognized: 'Slothfulness casts into a deep sleep, and an idle person will suffer hunger' (Prov. 19:15). In Genesis 2:21 Adam is put into a deep sleep while a rib is taken from him by God in order, we are told, to create Eve. The same kind of deep sleep is caused by laziness. This is not a reference to a quick nap but to the profound lethargy to which too much sleep leads. Such idleness and indolence will eventually result in hunger, for the person will not have enough energy to grow food or enough money to buy food. So we read that 'The sluggard buries his hand in the dish, and will not even bring it back to his mouth' (Prov. 19:24; cf. 26:15). This rather obscure proverb gets across the sheer inactivity of the lazy person – he is too lazy even to take his hand out of the communal eating dish (perhaps it is also being kept there out of gluttony) and hasn't even got the energy to lift his hand to his mouth. One has a vision of this person being so tired that he (or she!) falls asleep at the meal, like the dormouse at the Mad Hatter's tea party. There is a certain sarcastic humour here at the lazy person's expense!

Continuing this theme we read that 'The sluggard does not plough in the autumn; he will seek at harvest and have nothing' (Prov. 20:4). Once again laziness and food are related. The lazy person does not think ahead to the consequences of his inaction, so his failure to plough leads to an inability to harvest. He still expects to reap the rewards of the harvest and almost seems surprised when the obvious result of his inactivity comes to pass. This sluggard looks expectantly at harvest time in spite of not having done the necessary work. Some scholars have suggested that the sluggard referred to here has sown his seed but on unprepared ground that has not been properly ploughed. This might mean that he is genuinely surprised by his lack of harvest. This interpretation still gets across the point that if the soil is not prepared, the person concerned cannot expect to get as good a result as the person who has done everything necessary. The sluggard knows what goals he wishes to achieve, but is unwilling to put the time into achieving them. He desires good things but fails through his own indolence to provide for his livelihood – such a person is his own worse enemy! The lesson here is that it is no good sitting back and expecting things to come to you: the task must be carefully executed.

The sluggard is full of excuses for why he cannot work. For example, 'The sluggard says, "There is a lion outside! I shall be slain in the streets!"' (Prov. 22:13). This is rather like the boy who cried wolf – no one will listen to the person who goes on saying such things. They are absurd excuses and show the extent to which a lazy person will go to rationalize his desire to stay inside and rest. They are simply excuses for inactivity, evasive devices that hide the truth that he has a serious character defect! There is also an overtone that people who don't go out and don't interact with others, develop a vulnerability towards the world outside and feel afraid. This proverb, rather than simply being a maxim, manages in a very few words, to paint a vivid picture.

This same proverb is repeated in Proverbs 26 as part of a longer musing on the sluggard:

> The sluggard says, "There is a lion in the road!
>   There is a lion in the streets!"
> As a door turns on its hinges,
>   so does a sluggard on his bed.
> The sluggard buries his hand in the dish;
>   it wears him out to bring it back to his
>   mouth.
> The sluggard is wiser in his own eyes
>   than seven men who can answer
>   discreetly.
>
> (vv. 13–16)

This is, in fact, a repetition of two proverbs in that the man with his hand in the dish is back and once again he is too lacklustre even to bring the food to his mouth! It is clear that physical inactivity is being stressed here – notably the sheer inertia of the lazy person. The sluggard is most at home in bed. The image of a door is a clever parallel. When a door moves it doesn't go anywhere because it is anchored on its hinges. In similar fashion the sluggard is anchored to his bed: turning in bed is the maximum movement to which he aspires. He doesn't even get out of bed in order to move, but rather moves in a way that leads to not moving at all – this is the height of laziness, what might be termed 'getting laziness down to a fine art'! The sluggard also thinks he knows best. He is not used to listening to others or taking advice. Perhaps being in bed for so long he has had time to nourish his own illusions and has never had the opportunity to be disabused of his high opinion of himself and his wisdom. He secretly thinks that he is rather clever to be getting away with doing so little and does not realize that he has lost respect in the eyes of others. The reference to 'seven men who can answer discreetly' is simply to an indefinite number of people who do have common sense and hence have obtained real wisdom. Some scholars have suggested that the sluggard privately sees lying in bed as a higher form of wisdom in that by staying there he is avoiding trouble and enjoying life. This may be so, but at any rate it is an attitude of which the wise most certainly do not approve. This series of proverbs pokes fun at the lazy person and is intended to make such a person ashamed of himself and even stir him into action (if that is possible . . .)!

The message about work leading to prosperity is reiterated over and over again by the wise. They advocate productive action. In 'Love not sleep, lest you come to poverty; open your eyes, and you will have plenty of bread' (Prov. 20:13), a contrast is made between laziness and being wide awake and getting on with life. Sleeping will lead to a person losing his inheritance, but if he keeps his eyes open and stays alert and busy, he will never want. Since eyes are intended to be used in the daylight hours the person who spends most of the day asleep is going against the natural order of things and is courting disaster. But, the wise warn, don't try too hard: 'The plans of the diligent lead surely to abundance, but every one who is hasty comes only to want' (Prov 21:5). Here we have a warning against hastiness which is the antithesis to diligent planning. Planning and reflection lead to the careful and successful carrying out of a task whilst engaging in frenetic and hurried activity just leads to waste (see below pp. 56–65). There is a difference between hard work and being in too much of a hurry to get on in life. Hard work pays over a long period of time – it will bear its fruits slowly – but rushing into things will in the end prove unsatisfactory. Less haste and more thought is the message here.

Laziness brings shame not only on the individual but on his whole family. One person's actions have repercussions for others: 'A son who gathers in summer is prudent, but a son who sleeps in harvest brings shame' (Prov. 10:5). Neglect of proper attention to the harvest will lead to destitution and disgrace in the eyes of the whole community. The harvest was an occasion in the life of the community that demanded everyone's energies and, particularly as a family member, it was shameful to be in bed at such a time. Such behaviour could only have negative effects: 'Like vinegar to the teeth, and smoke to the eyes, so is the sluggard to those who send him' (Prov. 10:26). A bitter taste is left in the mouth of the person who recommends another in good faith, but he or she turns out to be lazy and inattentive and lets everyone down. What smoke, vinegar and lazy employees have in common is that they are irritants to the person experiencing their effects. Vinegar could refer to any acid drink made from grape juice which might be refreshing but more often than not can be quite unpleasant to drink. A sluggard is as sure to cause distress to an employer as vinegar is painful to the nerve endings of the teeth – an experience to which no doubt many of us can relate!

We have seen how the wise enjoyed the idea that life was a path which, if one behaved according to the right principles, was smooth and easy to walk along but which, if one upset the delicate order of things, would be beset with thorns or pitfalls. The same image occurs in connection with the theme of laziness: 'The way of a sluggard is overgrown with thorns, but the path of the upright is a level highway' (Prov. 15:19). The thorns in the way refer to obstacles or hindrances that people make for themselves, for example in their imaginary excuses for non-achievement. The more habitual their behaviour, the more insurmountable the obstacles become, with the result that little progress is made along life's path. But laziness is just one of many other less desirable traits which lead in the same direction. By contrast the confident person presses along a smooth path free from self-imposed obstacles.

In Proverbs 24 we find another extended section about laziness, this time in the form of a little story describing the process of learning and understanding on the part of the writer:

> I passed by the field of a sluggard,
>   by the vineyard of a man without sense;
> and lo, it was all overgrown with thorns;
>   the ground was covered with nettles,
>   and its stone wall was broken down.
> Then I saw and considered it;
>   I looked and received instruction.
> A little sleep, a little slumber,
>   a little folding of the hands to rest,
> and poverty will come upon you like a robber,
>   and want like an armed man.
>   (Prov. 24:30–4)

In this picture of land that has been so neglected that even the wall forming its boundary has fallen down, the thorns represent the growth that springs up in neglected places, making the ground unusable. How long will it be until its owner loses all he has? It teaches the writer the salutary lesson that a little sleep (the natural ally of sloth) soon leads to poverty. The 'folding of the hands to rest' refers to the preparations that one makes for sleep, such as lying down comfortably and composing oneself. Poverty is described here as a ruthless enemy which, if allowed to take hold, will destroy a person's very substance.

There are, in fact, more proverbs about the dangers of laziness than about work. Warnings against laziness, then, are more important to the sages than praise of the work ethic itself. Following their advice about the dangers of sloth, however, will automatically lead the wise person into worthwhile pursuit and activity which is what they are ultimately advocating. If only the lazy person would follow the example of the hard-working ant:

> Go to the ant, O sluggard,
>   consider her ways, and be wise.
> Without having any chief, officer or ruler,
>   she prepares her food in summer,
>   and gathers her sustenance in harvest.
> How long will you lie there, O sluggard?
>   When will you arise from your sleep?
>   (Prov. 6:6–9)

The advice of the sages is aimed primarily at young men (although we can extrapolate it for men and women of all ages) and we all know how adolescents like their beds – maybe that is why there is such an emphasis on this here!

These proverbs may lead us to reflect on the place of work in our own lives. Are we diligent? Are we happy in our work? Have we made the right choice of career? Do we ever trick our employer out of time that we should be spending working? How important is work (in the broadest sense and not necessarily a paid job) in relation to other aspects of our lives, and how far do we think about the balance between these different aspects? The proverbs on work certainly give us food for thought.

Money

> Money makes the world go round . . .
>   (*Cabaret*)

We live in an age in which how much money you have is a yardstick of success. If you have money you have status, you have security, you have power, you have freedom. The monied form their own class, regardless of background or education. Their money has often been hard won – the rich reward of hard work sometimes from an early age. We admire those who have been successful enough to acquire a substantial amount of money and who are able to lead the kind of life that no longer requires hard work. But we are less admiring of money that is not hard won but rather acquired as a hand-out or perhaps a lottery win.

The majority of people strive for a career that will ensure a secure financial future often undergoing rigorous training, or working long hours, or changing jobs regularly purely to achieve a better salary. This sometimes leads to dissatisfaction, causing people to step back and consider whether gain should be their only motivation, or whether they should seek to pursue a career they would really enjoy. There is often a conflict between pragmatism and idealism. Old loyalties are forgotten in the quest for cash. This *modus operandi* has become accepted in a world where only the fittest survive and the first requisite for that survival is money.

Many people would expect the Bible to be against the drive for money that characterizes our age and would be surprised to learn that in fact the Proverbs actually favour wealth. One of money's major benefits is the security it brings: 'A rich man's wealth is his strong city; the poverty of the poor is their ruin' (Prov. 10:15). The wise see the benefits of storing up money for a rainy day, of investing for the future so that a person has something to fall back on. Only fools spend all the money they earn and so have nothing put by to give them the security that they need. The image of a strong fortress, contrasted here with a ruined city, conveys the message that wealth protects against the chance happenings of life, while poverty destroys the poor, who are vulnerable and have no means to provide a margin of safety between themselves and potential disaster. Proverbs 18:11 reiterates this sentiment but this time without the contrast with the poor: 'A rich man's wealth is his strong city, and like a high wall protecting him', an image which puts me in mind of the high walls and gates lining the streets of Beverly Hills in Hollywood. Of course these high gates serve a double function – they not only indicate a stronghold of safety, but a desire for privacy on the part of the properties' owners and the means to afford to maintain it. But they also betray the fear that the owner may be a target because of his or her goods – a consideration that is always at the back of the mind of the person with many possessions. Wealth, then, is a buffer against danger and provides a protective enclosure, yet all the while with the inference that these walls are not as safe as the rich might think. They think that they can keep the world out, but can they?

Our nation is now in the grip of lottery-mania, and we hear stories about those who enjoy great wins and those who have just missed them. A large win receives a certain accolade, but it is rightly regarded as a matter of luck rather than skill. The wise were suspicious of easy money: 'Wealth hastily gotten will dwindle, but he who gathers little by little will increase it' (Prov. 13:11). The careful saver is preferred to the lottery winner. Hard, purposeful work confirms a person's character and worth and leads to lasting riches. The one who gets rich quickly and without effort may just as quickly lose it all again by reckless expenditure. Whilst few of us would turn our backs on a lottery win, the possibility has raised the question in many people's minds about whether they really would want to win after all. There would suddenly be no point in working which might lead to a certain amount of boredom; so much money would bring responsibility and possible unpleasant repercussions, such as unwanted publicity and begging letters; it would also cut one off from friends who didn't enjoy the same kind of wealth. I have personally heard of a number of people who started doing the lottery with great fervour but who are actually secretly rather glad that they have not won! It seems that the slow and steady saving route is perhaps the more realistic and ultimately more secure.

The responsibilities of money are brought out by the wise in a proverb which speaks about ransom: 'The ransom of a man's life is his wealth, but a poor man has no means of redemption' (Prov. 13:8). I take this to mean that wealth becomes a weapon that others can use against a person. While there is little point in holding a person who has nothing to ransom, there is every point in the case of those who are wealthy, and presumably such threats would be impossible to ignore. So the rich have to live with this vulnerability while the poor at least do not have this worry. One might decide on the basis of this interpretation that it is better to be poor – but this is not a conclusion the wise usually come to. Faced with such a situation the rich person might ask, 'Why should my hard-won money simply be taken away from me by a lunatic?' This is true – such an action would be grossly unfair, and yet in a world of 'haves' and 'have nots', there will always be the threat that the 'have-nots' will try to grasp the possessions of the 'haves'. Another slightly more positive way of interpreting this proverb, and one more in line with the usual commendation of the wise that wealth is a good thing, is to say that the rich have the benefit of being able to ransom their own lives if necessary, while the poor cannot. Thus the poor person is at a disadvantage and has no shield from insecurity. So perhaps it is better to have money after all! The basic point is that, either way, money creates differences between rich and poor and, depending on which way you look at it, one group can seem better off than the other.

So, in the eyes of the wise, wealth is to be striven for, since, after all, rich people have many friends: 'The poor is disliked even by his neighbour, but the rich has many friends' (Prov. 14:20). Of course, this could be interpreted as a slightly pointed remark about the fact that rich people can attract false friends who are only interested in spending their money, but this is not in fact the dominant sense here. It is rather that the poor person has not striven in the way that he might have done and so has not reaped the benefits of successful interaction with others and has not built worthwhile friendships. Even his neighbour, from whom sympathy might be expected since he lives in close relation and proximity, has been alienated presumably by the poor man's demands on him – financial or otherwise – which have instilled resentment and hatred in him. The proverb is highlighting the fact that riches create differences in social life, and that wealth and popularity are often linked. The rich person makes no demands on his friends – they stand only to gain from his generous hospitality. This sense is also brought out in another proverb: 'Wealth brings many new friends, but a poor man is deserted by his friend' (Prov. 19:4). When a friendship becomes burdensome, the close bonds that hold the friendship together may eventually be cut. Social inequity, we are being told, often leads to problems and the hardships of the poor lead ironically to the build-up of resentment and further distress. Another proverb has these hard words to say about poverty: 'All a poor man's brothers hate him; how much more do his friends go far from him! He pursues them with words, but does not have them' (Prov. 19:7). The point here is that brothers have a duty that friends don't have. Families tend to stick around through the good times and the bad. Friends, on the other hand, can drop someone who becomes burdensome and can erect barriers to destroy the old intimacies. So if you are in the position that even your own family don't like you, you are less likely to have any friends!

But the wise have a word of warning for those who think it is fine to sit and watch their rising bank balance: only the rich person who uses his wealth in the right way is to be admired, such as the philanthropist, for example. 'One man gives freely, yet grows all the richer; another withholds what he should give, and only suffers want. A liberal man will be enriched, and one who waters will himself be watered' (Prov. 11:24–5). Although this proverb could simply be an observation of the fact that things don't always turn out as expected, it seems to have a more moral purpose urging a person towards generosity rather than stinginess. The first rule for the wealthy is generosity to those less fortunate than themselves. Those who give freely will become richer; those who are mean will themselves end up poor. The reference here may be to both a material and a spiritual richness, or conversely poverty. A person whose generosity is a source of blessing to others will in turn enjoy prosperity. Furthermore, the rich can sleep soundly in their beds if they know that they have not turned their back on those in need. Of course it is not being advocated that all should be given away, simply that a person should exercise a healthy philanthropy and show kindness: 'He who is kind to the poor lends to the Lord, and he will repay him for his deed' (Prov. 19:17). Kindness is seen to be an act that pleases God and for which a person will be rewarded. Generosity is here seen as a form of lending to God, so putting God in debt and ensuring that he will surely reward the giver. The converse is also true: ignoring the poor will eventually lead to misery: 'He who closes his ear to the cry of the poor will himself cry out and not be heard' (Prov. 21:13). This is not a message of giving all one has to the poor: the wise were far too pragmatic for that. But helping the poor is regarded as a duty – you might after all find yourself in the same situation one day. Those who do not show mercy will indeed not be helped in their day of need.

So, the power and influence that comes with wealth has to be properly wielded in favour of helping those less fortunate and in setting a good example to others. In fact the acquisition of wealth is not to be an end in itself – it is worthless unless it is accompanied by fitting behaviour: 'A good name is to be chosen rather than great riches, and favour is better than silver or gold' (Prov. 22:1). Here the wise have moved beyond the benefits of wealth to a consideration of its relative value. Responsibly managed, wealth is seen to be a good thing which comes as a reward for righteousness. However, reputation is preferable to wealth and personal qualities are better than riches. The message is that wealth is attainable and useful, but it does not by itself command respect. More important is, rather, acceptance by others, and whilst wealth may assist that process it is not an end in itself. According to the wise, then, wealth needs to be set within a wider framework of values that lead to a full life: without that framework, wealth is a snare.

Wealth brings power – that is a fact of life: 'The rich rules over the poor, and the borrower is the slave of the lender' (Prov. 22:7). How true this particular proverb rings in the ears of anyone with a mortgage! There is no getting away from the fact that money breeds money and that much money is made from the exploitation of others. Debt is a form of slavery in that it makes the borrower dependent on the lender, so depriving him or her of personal independence. This is a warning not to fall into serious debt! The wise recognized the power of money as a fact. They sought to shape the underlying attitudes of the rich and the poor. Since there will always be the rich and poor, the issue is teaching people how to use rather than abuse money and how therefore to make being wealthy meaningful. They utter the stern warning: 'He who oppresses the poor to increase his own wealth, or gives to the rich, will only come to want' (Prov. 22:16). This curious proverb is open to different translations, but the meaning seems to be that gaining wealth by impropriety is wrong and giving to the rich (to curry favour perhaps) is a pointless activity. Wealth needs to be carefully won and carefully preserved – unfair accumulation and squandering only lead to poverty.

God is not seen to be either on the side of rich or poor: he rewards the deeds of both. The poor are criticized for their sloth and lack of motivation and the rich praised for their prudence and philanthropy. However, the wise recognize that the poor are more vulnerable than the rich in that they do not have the resources to obtain justice for themselves. So, in cases of mistreatment of the poor by the rich, God is on the side of the poor: 'Do not rob the poor, because he is poor, or crush the afflicted at the gate; for the Lord will plead their cause and despoil of life those who despoil them' (Prov. 22:22–3). God takes the part of the oppressed and fights for them. 'At the gate' refers to being in court and the act of despoiling could well refer to the seizure of the property of debtors in order to pay off their debts. Ill treatment of other people, especially those in a low social position who are hence defenceless, will have repercussions: 'He who oppresses a poor man insults his Maker, but he who is kind to the needy honours him' (Prov. 14:31). In other words to maltreat a person is to insult God, whilst to recognize that person as a human being in need and help them is to honour God. It is a common experience that if we wrong someone we are eaten up with guilt and we cannot rest until the wrong is righted. God is in a sense our conscience – he is on the side of justice.

Poor people who oppress other poor people are equally criticized: 'A poor man who oppresses the poor is a beating rain that leaves no food' (Prov. 28:3). Just as one might expect rain to be a blessing which enables the earth to produce food, in its violent form it does the opposite by spoiling crops and fruit and causing famine. So it is when a poor person, rather than showing sympathy, is merciless.

In a society where robbery and cheating of customers was clearly widespread, the wise regarded the poor stealing from the poor as particularly unsatisfactory. Integrity was all important: 'Better is a poor man who walks in his integrity than a rich man who is perverse in his ways' (Prov. 28:6). Poverty with spiritual wholeness and integrity is better than wealth with perversion and depravity. In their view a moral way of life is of far greater value than any amount of money. In the ideal world of the Wisdom writers the person of integrity has riches, whereas in reality the rich sometimes lack such integrity and the poor sometimes have more insight. There is a hint here that the 'black and white' view of the world in which righteousness is rewarded doesn't always match up with reality, a matter about which Job so often complains. But we are told that, even when things do not seem fair, God knows what is really in our hearts. Ultimately wealth will not enable a rich man to escape the consequences of his evil deeds. Thus, 'Riches do not profit in the day of wrath, but righteousness delivers from death' (Prov. 11:4). At the end of the day, it is clear that good morals matter more than riches. Wealth without righteousness can never protect against God's judgement. Righteousness is the only path of life which guarantees long life over against premature death.

There are warnings against the wealthy becoming arrogant or wise in their own eyes. Because wealth brings power and authority, it can lead to bossiness and authoritarianism: 'A rich man is wise in his own eyes, but a poor man who has understanding will find him out' (Prov. 28:11). This kind of wrong behaviour is easily exposed by one whose eyes have not been blinded by money or success and it is ironic that the wise man who has become rich can all too easily become wise in his own eyes, i.e. too full of his own achievement. Riches may lead to confidence, but wisdom doesn't always accompany wealth. The poor man with his religious insight can see the flaws in his rich counterpart and has the measure of him. There is perhaps something of this message against pride and arrogance in the rich in the rather strange proverb: 'The poor use entreaties, but the rich answer roughly' (Prov. 18:23). Since money talks, the rich can afford to speak their mind. But the poor have to watch their tongues too lest they be rebuffed. In this sense speech betrays social class. Social eminence and rudeness of manner are associated with wealth, whilst humility and ingratiating talk are associated with poverty. The rich person may have developed a brusque manner in responding to the hard-luck stories of the poor, i.e. it might partly be a defence mechanism. However, it is true that the discernment that accompanied the initial success of a person can all too often be lost when he or she has become successful and wealthy.

The proverbs warn against people who seem to be what they are not and this is very much the case with wealth and poverty. 'One man pretends to be rich, yet has nothing; another pretends to be poor, yet has great wealth' (Prov. 13:7). This proverb reminds me of a poor person, who, in order to try and find himself or herself a rich partner, circulates with the wealthy, going to all their parties and posing as rich in order to appear what he or she is not. The converse is also true – it is impossible to know what people have stored away in their bank accounts. A person who seems to have lived a very simple and limited life can in death be revealed to have been a millionaire! Money is known to do strange things to people and attitudes to money can be damaging to relationships. The element of pretence in this proverb shows how perverse human nature can be, as well as the very different approaches that people have to money. It also sends the message that true wealth does not consist in worldly goods, i.e. money does not define a person and provides little insight about the quality of a person. In fact, one should not judge by appearances, for although a person may affect ostentation, in reality he may have nothing, while another person with money stored up in the bank may behave as if he were penniless. Both types of unbalanced and immoderate behaviour are con-

demned by the wise. The wise liked balance and
equilibrium in life – they were against extremism of any
kind. They also didn't like people who concealed their true
nature. And they didn't like excess – too much spending
and too much over-indulgence could put the rich man back
in the poorhouse: 'He who loves pleasure will be a poor
man; he who loves wine and oil will not be rich' (Prov.
21:17). Spendthrift behaviour such as that indulged in by
people who love festivities and extravagant and luxurious
living will ultimately lead to poverty. Wealth does not come
to the idle and pleasure-loving but to the diligent. Those
who seek primarily the enjoyment of wealth instead of
virtuous living will not prosper in the end.

Wealth, then, is a mixed blessing. Some proverbs regard
too much fixation on the acquisition of wealth as unhealthy:
'Do not toil to acquire wealth; be wise enough to desist.
When your eyes light upon it, it is gone; for suddenly it
takes to itself wings, flying like an eagle toward heaven'
(Prov. 23:4–5). Money is not the steady rock some take it
to be – it is a security, yes, but not one which can be
trusted absolutely. Only God is to be trusted absolutely.
Wealth is ephemeral, fickle and unpredictable, and so it is
senseless to wear oneself out trying to obtain it or being
anxious about it. It is here today and gone tomorrow and
often hopelessly out of reach, as distant as an eagle in the
sky. All too often money is fleeting, especially when hastily
acquired: 'A faithful man will abound with blessings, but he
who hastens to be rich will not go unpunished' (Prov.
28:20). Because of their haste to be rich some people act
precipitously and without reflection, and end up doing what
is evil. Wisdom is about getting one's priorities right:
those who put their responsibilities to others first will be
comfortably off, but those who put greed and ambition first
will come to a bad end. The wise were very suspicious of
get-rich-quick schemes! All too often, they say, the pursuit
of wealth distracts from the more important aspects of life

such as faithfulness and kindness. 'A miserly man hastens after wealth, and does not know that want will come upon him' (Prov. 28:22). Of course it is very true that wealthy people are often miserly because they are intent upon increasing their wealth and they have probably had to be penny-pinching in the past in order to accumulate it in the first place. Here misers are seen as hurrying towards wealth: they are blind to their own folly and do not realize that the final result of their actions will be penury. Such a person is unfit for the responsibility that wealth brings. The wise hated miserliness: 'Do not eat the bread of a man who is stingy; do not desire his delicacies; for he is like one who is inwardly reckoning. "Eat and drink!" he says to you; but his heart is not with you' (Prov. 23:6–7). The hospitality a miser provides is hollow: he does not mean what he says but rather begrudges you the food on your plate. Such people are best avoided!

At the end of the day, the wise recognized the importance of money and thought that the gradual acquisition of wealth was a good thing as long as it was accompanied by a generous and giving attitude. Love is more important than money. As it says in the deeply insightful proverb: 'Better is a dinner of herbs where love is than a fatted ox and hatred with it' (15:17). It is not riches that make for love, but people; it is better to be poor and loved than rich and hated. Wealth brings its own pitfalls and it is certainly ephemeral in nature. The author of Proverbs 30, who enjoys numbering, can pray to be neither rich nor poor but simply provided for by God. He wishes to be protected from liars and from excessive poverty or wealth so that he has enough but not too much as to become arrogant and forgetful of God, and not too little that he resorts to stealing. He recognizes that both unjust conduct and extremes of wealth or poverty could lead to infidelity: a life which is too easy leads to the illusion of self-sufficiency that does not need God, while a life of destitution will easily result in sin. All this writer wants is the necessities of life so that there is no danger of offending God nor any incentive to evil behaviour. His prayer focuses on the need for divine help to gain the moral character that will enable him to be true to his religious faith and an honest way of life, rather than on material things. It is unusual among the collection of proverbs for its expression of piety. In essence it calls for balance in life:

> Two things I ask of thee;
>> deny them not to me before I die:
> Remove far from me falsehood and lying;
>> give me neither poverty nor riches;
>> feed me with the food that is needful for me,
> lest I be full, and deny thee,
>> and say, 'Who is the Lord?'
> or lest I be poor, and steal,
>> and profane the name of my God.
>
> (Prov. 30:7–9)

Planning for good or ill

> 'I have a cunning plan . . .'
>> (Baldrick in *Blackadder*)

Planning is a less obvious theme for Proverbs but it is one upon which the wise place a good deal of emphasis. In the realms of work or money, planning is the key to success. A well-planned career will succeed in a way that a haphazard one is unlikely to, and planning for one's future is an essential part of the good handling of money. The wise recognized the importance of planning not just in these areas but in all areas of one's life. Without planning, there is a danger of the onset of chaos. When you have planned well, you are on much firmer ground in that you know in which direction you are heading.

A key part of planning is consultation with others. In the words of the wise we find a recognition that, as the English proverb expresses it, 'Two heads are better than one'. So we read: 'Without counsel plans go wrong, but with many advisers they succeed' (Prov. 15:22). Without prior consultation even the best laid plans fall apart. When the opinions of others are taken on board, they are able to own the plan that is put on the table for consideration. If a number of advisers are involved in shaping a policy it is more likely to succeed. This is the best argument for a committee that I have ever heard! In similar vein we also read: 'Plans are established by counsel; by wise guidance wage war' (Prov. 20:18). Here we can imagine a context of advisers to the king giving their considered and combined advice after careful planning. This underlines the key role of strategy in a war situation (cf. Prov. 24:6) and, even if the reference to war is figurative and it really refers to the struggle to succeed in daily life, strategy is needed here too. It is better not to leave things to chance but to plan in detail and if possible in consultation with others: 'Where there is no guidance, a people falls; but in an abundance of counsellors there is safety' (Prov. 11:14). It is probable that the wise were employed in the processes of decision-making and giving advice, and so these proverbs sound rather like a justification of a key part of their own role. Good planning leads to inspired decisions for all.

One person who is especially adept at dealing out good decisions is the king: 'Inspired decisions are on the lips of a king; his mouth does not sin in judgement' (Prov. 16:10). The king was the ultimate authority and leader, especially gifted in decision-making and legal judgements with powers that were regarded as divinely endowed. However, if he didn't take the advice of others, he was equally in danger of going off the path of wisdom and being misled by his sense of his own greatness.

There is a strong recognition of the role of God in planning too: 'The plans of the mind belong to man, but the answer of the tongue is from the Lord . . . Commit your work to the Lord, and your plans will be established' (Prov. 16:1, 3). This is an acknowledgement of God's will for individuals and of the fact that, when human plans are not in accordance with his will, they will not be implemented. It is not intended to belittle human decision-making but to indicate human dependence on God for the successful execution of plans. It also underlines the all-seeing and all-powerful nature of God and his interaction with the world. Sometimes we all recognize that we make unrealistic plans or ones that we know are not in our best interests or those of others. The second half of this proverb encourages us to trust in God and not be secretive; we need to resign ourselves to God's will and try to plan and live in harmony with it. We so often forget the divine dimension in decision-making – the power of prayer and of taking 'counsel' with God. We cannot always rely on intellectual decisions – sometimes we just have a 'gut feeling' about something. Emotional decisions that come from the heart are often more true to ourselves than cold rational ones. The wise felt that human plans were safe in God's hands, but that left to the individuals themselves the process was very uncertain. There is an important interaction here between human devising and human advice and the sanctioning of such plans by God. The wise caution: 'Many are the plans in the mind of a man, but it is the purpose of the Lord that will be established' (Prov. 19:21). It is interesting that God's 'purpose' is in the singular: he is able to see the whole picture, the totality of our lives, whereas we, with each plan, only see our lives in chunks. God's intention for us, therefore, is much larger than any of us can comprehend. There is a delicate interplay then between the human realm and the realm of God. In this last proverb it could be argued that there is an element of destiny, i.e. that God has a plan for every person's life which ensures the desired outcome.

Of course there are problems with this kind of viewpoint when we come to issues such as suffering. It is all very well for God to intend good things for us, but what about bad things? Does he intend these to happen? It is great when our decisions are in harmony with God's will, but there is sometimes disharmony, such as Job experienced and as implied in this proverb: 'A man's mind plans his way, but the Lord directs his steps' (Prov. 16:9). Again a distinction is made between the whole direction of our lives as purposed by God and our own decision-making. We are so used to making our own decisions in life that we find it hard to see God as directing our steps. Maybe we need to think about stepping back and trusting God, allowing him to work in our lives. There is a certain element of luck and chance in the whole process of which the wise were aware. Sometimes people throw a coin into the air and see where it lands to help them to make a decision. This is, it seems, nothing new for we read: 'The lot is cast into the lap, but the decision is wholly from the Lord' (Prov. 16:33). However, whilst human beings may think that chance is coming into play, this proverb tells us that in fact God is the one making the decisions. Human decisions that seem to us to be arbitrary are actually from God. He is ultimately in control.

A related issue is that of planning to do evil, or calculated dishonesty. This is an issue against which the wise rage vehemently. The weighing of goods either with false weights or crooked scales was a common trick in ancient Israel, with the result that people were paying for less than they thought they were getting. It is rather like the repackaging of products so that they become smaller and smaller in size even though the price remains the same –

none of us are fooled, although we may go on buying things out of habit. So we read: 'A false balance is an abomination to the Lord, but a just weight is his delight' (Prov. 11:1). The condemnation is strong – clearly such falsity was regarded as a serious crime, a direct offence against God and the divine order. Proverbs 20:23 is equally damning: 'Diverse weights are an abomination to the Lord, and false scales are not good.' Honest communication amongst human beings is essential, hence the condemnation of this dishonest behaviour. God is on the side of right and of just treatment of others: 'A just balance and scales are the Lord's; all the weights in the bag are his work' (Prov. 16:11). God claims ownership of justice – it is part of the created order and hence of the social order that should be adhered to by human beings. Scales and weights are seen here as instruments of divine justice. Similar remarks are made about false measures, referring perhaps to dry measures of grain and the like: 'Diverse weights and diverse measures are both alike an abomination to the Lord' (Prov. 20:10).

Another trick devised by these crafty schemers is persuading others to give surety for money or goods, i.e. promising support for someone who is trying to secure a loan and being ultimately liable if that person is unable to pay it back. The wise were not in favour of such activity: 'He who gives surety for a stranger will smart for it, but he who hates suretyship is secure' (Prov. 11:15). The wise thought that such behaviour not only compromised a person's own financial security but also his or her peace of mind (cf. Prov. 6:1–5 for a longer piece on this subject). Giving surety for a stranger might seem odd to us, but this in fact refers to anyone not in one's immediate family or group of friends, an acquaintance perhaps. Another proverb on the same subject states: 'A man without sense gives a pledge, and becomes surety in the presence of his neighbour' (Prov. 17:18). The neighbour is there as a witness which means that the individual who has guaranteed the money cannot escape from the transaction as his own honesty would be on the line if he did not honour the financial commitment made. The message here is that it is wiser to take charge of your own affairs than to become involved in someone else's and get your hands burnt.

The wise had a strong sense of self-preservation. They were against undue risk and against compromising one's personal freedom. To underwrite the financial liabilities of another was, they thought, to court ruin. The advice of the wise to the lender of the money in this situation, then, is to take some security from the person for whom he has given surety in order to guarantee repayment, especially when dealing with anyone in a high risk group such as a stranger or a foreigner: 'Take a man's garment when he has given surety for a stranger, and hold him in pledge when he gives surety for foreigners' (Prov. 20:16; cf. Prov. 27:13). However, pledges are best avoided: 'Be not one of those who give pledges, who become surety for debts. If you have nothing with which to pay, why should your bed be taken from under you?' (Prov. 22:26–7). Trying to extract money from a person who has no money at the end of a loan period can only cause problems. Having to send the bailiffs in to take the bed from under a person is not very charitable and is certainly destructive to any friendship! In today's world we hardly think twice about borrowing and lending. The personal aspect of it has gone, now that the risks are taken by large banks and insurance companies which are much less vulnerable in such situations than individuals. However, these warnings underline the uncertain nature of such activity and are a warning against getting ourselves too far into the hands and pockets of others.

A third trick was withholding goods in order to push the price up and then selling at a premium: 'The people curse him who holds back grain, but a blessing is on the head of him who sells it' (Prov. 11:26). While the less scrupulous might regard such action as sound economic activity, the wise were of the opinion that the quest for personal gain at the expense of others was wrong and that people would be blessed by God if they sold their grain to relieve the distress of others. Social responsibility weighed heavily on the wise. Related to this is the scam of pretending that a thing is worthless and then selling it for much more. This reminds me of a Roald Dahl story in which a dealer comes to the house of a man who is in possession of a priceless antique table. The dealer does not let on about its worth but pretends it is worthless and that he is doing the man a favour by taking it away. Whilst the dealer's back is turned the man, on having difficulty getting the antique table into the car, chops off the legs, saying, 'Well, it won't matter since it is just going to the scrapheap.' Imagine the dealer's alarm! So we read: '"It is bad, it is bad," says the buyer; but when he goes away, then he boasts' (Prov. 20:14). In this proverb, which recreates the lively scene of the Eastern market-place with its haggling and bargaining, the buyer thinks that he has won a bargain and cheated the seller. It is a warning not to be taken in by crafty buyers! There are all kinds of pitfalls for the unsuspecting person wanting to engage in business transactions – these proverbs flag up the reality of the tricks that people play on others for their own gain. The wise advocate that it is better to be charitable and generous to others in society than to work only for personal gain. In fact God will ultimately prevent unjust dealers from enjoying their ill-gotten gains: 'He who augments his wealth by interest and increase gathers it for him who is kind to the poor' (Prov. 28:8). Ultimately, says this proverb, good will prevail. The needs of the poor should not be an occasion for commercial gain, rather the better-off have a duty to help them.

Bribing is another crafty practice: 'A bribe is like a magic stone in the eyes of him who gives it; wherever he turns he prospers' (Prov. 17:8). This proverb makes it seem that bribing is good since it opens doors. The wise recognized that there was a subtle distinction between giving a gift to secure a favour or as a present to a ruler, and bribery with malevolent intent. In this proverb, then, giving gifts or bribes is regarded as beneficial, at least in the eyes of the person who gives them. The wise are making an observation about the realities of life and human interaction. However, 'in the eyes of him who gives it' indicates their slight reservation: inevitably such a gift has a distorting effect. It gives its initiator a feeling of power, but there is something illusory about it. Although it apparently succeeds, it could rebound with bad consequences. And bribes can certainly be used for ill: 'A wicked man accepts a bribe from the bosom to pervert the ways of justice' (Prov. 17:23). Anyone who deals with bribes runs the danger of finding himself caught up with the wrong kinds of people. It is better to give a gift out of genuine generosity than a bribe: 'A man's gift makes room for him and brings him before great men' (Prov. 18:16). A gift can be a polite gesture which can be used to smooth one's way in life and as such can be very beneficial. The wise were pragmatists: they considered it was better to pay off an angry person behind closed doors to prevent them making a scene in public, so, for example: 'A gift in secret averts anger; and a bribe in the bosom, strong wrath' (Prov. 21:14). The wise recognized that bribery can work and that shrewd behaviour leads to success and influence. They also didn't like anger, and so anything that was a palliative to potential anger was a good thing. This sort of behaviour reminds me of the lobbying that goes on behind the scenes in parliament or of the role of the business lunch in buttering up the client. It is not bad – and everybody does it – but since it can easily be misused it has to be handled cautiously and carefully.

Thus, the wise teach us that it is important to plan – and clearly planning for good purposes is preferable to planning for ill. Certainly the wise are not in favour of just letting

life drift and having no sense of future planning. It is part of
their sense of order that actions and words need to be
carefully thought through. Careful planning takes the stress
out of situations and enables one to know in which direction
one is going. However, having done our part, the wise
recognize that ultimately God plans our way and that we
can merely try our best to tune into his will for us.

I would like to end this section with a longer musing
from the wise in the language of shepherding and farming
on the importance of forward planning:

> Know well the condition of your flocks,
>   and give attention to your herds;
> for riches do not last for ever;
>   and does a crown endure to all
>   generations?
> When the grass is gone, and the new growth
>   appears,
>   and the herbage of the mountains is
>   gathered,
> the lambs will provide your clothing
>   and the goats the price of a field;
> there will be enough goats' milk for your
>   food,
>   for the food of your household
>   and maintenance for your maidens.
>   (Prov. 27:23–7)

The wise felt that farming was the best means of livelihood
as it provided a stable living, a self-contained way of life
and enduring wealth that could be passed down from one
generation to another. They were cautious of the more
volatile world of business. But they sounded the note of
caution that even a stable job needs to be nurtured –
continuing hard work is a necessity as a farm does not look
after itself and time does not stand still. One cannot rest on

one's laurels. Careful planning ensures that the good times can help to cope with the bad, rather like the biblical story of the seven years of plenty and the seven years of famine so successfully managed by Joseph (Gen. 41). The message is: store whilst there is plenty so that there is a reserve for times of hardship.

Emotive issues

> Don't worry, be happy . . .
>
> (Bobby McFerrin)

Pride

A key theme of Jane Austen's famous novel, *Pride and Prejudice*, is the barrier which pride erects to the acknowledgement of true feelings, made all the worse when it comes up against prejudice. While a dignified pride has its place, it can very often be destructive, as the wise are quick to point out: 'When pride comes, then comes disgrace; but with the humble is wisdom' (Prov. 11:2). It is hard to be humble. In the view of the wise those who are proud basically overestimate themselves, whilst those who are humble have a much truer evaluation of themselves. It is ironic that the proud seek honour but just get dishonour, whilst the modest person who does not seek honour receives it on account of his or her modesty. For the wise sincerity was very important, and so we read: 'Better is a man of humble standing who works for himself than one who plays the great man but lacks bread' (Prov. 12:9). This proverb continues the theme of pride over against humility but brings in additional elements of honesty and dishonesty. The self-effacing person without airs and graces who just presses on earning an honest living is praised above one who pretends to be what he or she is not. It is much better to be a person of small means who is content with his or her lot than to have delusions of affluence and live beyond one's means. This has social implications: a person of lower social status may well have more substance than a person with social prestige who tries to impress others whilst in reality starving at home.

In another proverb, 'Before destruction a man's heart is haughty, but humility goes before honour' (Prov. 18:12); the inference is that the proud will never admit that they are wrong but go on maintaining their pretence until the last moment. However, honour comes to the person who least expects it and who has a befitting humility. Pride and haughtiness are closely associated in the minds of the sages: 'Haughty eyes and a proud heart, the lamp of the wicked, are sin' (Prov. 21:4). A great deal about a person can be deduced from his or her manner. Haughtiness, pride and arrogance cannot be the basis of anything enduring, in fact they are the life-blood of sin. These character defects are typical of the 'scoffers' referred to in Proverbs 21:24: '"Scoffer" is the name of the proud, haughty man who acts with arrogant pride.' A 'scoffer' disregards the opinions of others, is unteachable and self-righteous, and disregards the moral law. Finally, 'Pride goes before destruction, and a haughty spirit before a fall. It is better to be of a lowly spirit with the poor than to divide the spoil with the proud' (Prov 16:18–19). A tension emerges here with which the wise were clearly wrestling. Although riches were usually the reward for good behaviour and those who were rich were also supposed to be wise, there were clearly those who were wealthy and wicked. In this case, poverty is held up as a better option. In fact, humility was more likely to be found amongst poor people. The message keeps coming across that virtue should precede everything else: if it makes a person wealthy then all well and good, but the material rewards should not become ends in themselves. 'To divide the spoil with the proud' is a reference to the practice of taking home the spoils of war. In this proverb's reference to the proud sharing the profits out between them there is an inference of ill-gotten gain – it is better, say the wise, not to partake in this greed.

God is seen ultimately to be against the proud person: 'The Lord tears down the house of the proud, but maintains the widow's boundaries' (Prov. 15:25). God is on the side of the underdog but only where it is deserved. He will bring down those who are proud and who do not help the poor; he will tear down their houses whilst protecting the property of the vulnerable. In situations where there was no male head of the household such as in the case of a widow, there was a feeling of great vulnerability. It is interesting that the king – the usual upholder of the rights of the poor on earth – is not mentioned here but rather God is held directly responsible for seeing that justice is done. Pride will in the end lead to nothing: 'A man's pride will bring him low, but he who is lowly in spirit will obtain honour' (Prov. 29:23). Humility, combined with due respect for God, will bring its own rewards. Here lies the road to life: 'The reward for humility and fear of the Lord is riches and honour and life' (Prov. 22:4).

Anger

The play *Look Back in Anger* by John Osborne was part of the 'angry young man' movement of the theatre in the 1950s. It portrays a man of, at times, uncontrollable temper who disrupts relationships and makes life difficult for all around him. This is tempered by a penitent childishness that never-theless endears those close to him and creates a bond that is deep and profound, the other side of the intense anger coin. The wise were aware of the dangers of a quick temper and so commend measured reactions. It seems they were not against the whole principle of anger, presumably con-sidering it justified in certain circumstances. There are a number of warnings against a hot temper: 'A man of quick temper acts foolishly, but a man of discretion is patient' (Prov. 14:17). Patience is a virtue, as is the tranquillity of mind and self-control that accompany it: 'He who is slow to anger has great understanding, but he who has a hasty temper exalts folly. A tranquil mind gives life to the flesh, but passion makes the bones rot' (Prov. 14:29–30). It is seen as wise to be slow to anger as well as slow to judge. A person who cannot be goaded into an unwise course of action has great insight, but he who acts hastily, reacting in anger to a situation, is seen to be on the path of folly. Calmness and control of anger are definitely recommended. Tranquillity, mental calmness and repose are seen to affect one's physical health for the better, whilst the passion of jealousy leads to sickness and disquiet which adversely affects the whole person. There is a recognition of the power of the mind over physical illness here and a concern for harmony on both an individual and societal level. A quick temper is seen to lead to violence: 'A hot-tempered man stirs up strife, but he who is slow to anger quiets contention' (Prov. 15:18). Anger is quickly communicated to others and leads to potential hostility, but lack of strife promotes peaceful living.

The wise advise against associating with angry people, 'Make no friendship with a man given to anger, nor go with a wrathful man, lest you learn his ways and entangle your-self in a snare' (Prov. 22:24–5). Anger is clearly catching and is the path to ensnarement and death. Impetuous behaviour and heated words were anathema to the wise who saw the angry person as unreasonable and incapable of dialogue. It is certainly true that anger tends to breed anger: 'A man of wrath stirs up strife, and a man given to anger causes much transgression' (Prov. 29:22). Angry people bring trouble upon themselves and others. Anger gets you nowhere – it just causes quarrelling and offence. In the explosive moment of anger all understanding and communication break down and the injury caused can be lasting.

Some proverbs specifically concern the wrath of the king. When anger is accompanied by power this clearly endangers the lives and well-being of others. In the proverb, 'A king's wrath is a messenger of death, and a wise man will appease it' (Prov. 16:14), there is the suggestion that the king's anger can sometimes be irrational. Anger is the enemy of good decisions and can threaten a person's career and prospects. One of the skills a courtier needs is to be able to keep the king happy. In fact, not being quick to rise to anger and being able to exercise self-control successfully is considered such a virtue that it is seen as better even than military prowess: 'He who is slow to anger is better than the mighty, and he who rules his spirit than he who takes a city' (Prov. 16:32). Wisdom is better than brute force. The wise understood that controlling one's temper is difficult but commend the wisdom of doing so: 'Good sense makes a man slow to anger, and it is his glory to overlook an offence. A king's wrath is like the growling of a lion, but his favour is like dew upon the grass' (Prov. 19:11–12). Here two proverbs on anger are placed side by side. The first reiterates the importance of controlling anger and adds that it is better to overlook a misdeed altogether and thus avoid an argument than to get angry about it. How often do we look back on an occasion, having calmed down after being angry and seen the whole incident in a new perspective, and been made to feel rather foolish? Or, having argued to win our point, how often have we felt a lack of glory in the winning? In the view of the wise it is better to bite one's tongue and not start the argument in the first place. The second proverb makes the point that, since the anger or favour of the king is more significant than that of other people, it is better to keep on the right side of him if possible! No one can afford to anger the king, for the consequences can be fatal. The same sentiment is reiterated in Proverbs 20:2: 'The dread wrath of a king is like the growling of a lion; he who provokes him to anger forfeits his life.' On this occasion there is no mention of favour, but rather a warning of the danger of losing one's life.

A strange little proverb is found in Proverbs 19:19: 'A man of great wrath will pay the penalty; for if you deliver him, you will only have to do it again.' Anyone who intervenes to try to help an angry person will discover that the same thing will only happen over and over again. A hasty temper can become a habit. People who have a problem with anger are therefore best avoided since they do not learn their lesson; they are dominated by the emotion and realistically there is no way of helping them. The wise then were very wary of those who are quick-tempered and were aware of the negative effects that anger can have. They recommended that the angry person should exercise control, if possible, and they warned the person on the receiving end of the need to beware, especially when dealing with anyone in authority.

Hopes, fears, joys and sorrows

The heart was considered by the wise to be the seat of the emotions, not to be confused with the spirit which, like the soul, spoke of the essence of a person. A number of proverbs speak of the heart, describing how it can be either bitter or joyful and affected by internal emotions as well as by external relationships. They often involve a contrast between being happy and sad. For example, one proverb tells us: 'Anxiety in a man's heart weighs him down, but a good word makes him glad' (Prov. 12:25). It is so often the case that the right word spoken by another can give us a new perspective on a problem or make us realize that our anxiety was unfounded. It is not only good for our own well-being to be cheerful, but it is good to be able to communicate cheerfully to others. The wise knew the power of genuine sympathy and pastoral concern for others. This proverb draws a contrast between internal worries which can so often get out of proportion and a reassuring or kindly word from outside that lifts the spirits. We know nowadays how damaging the effects of stress are to our bodily organs. The anxious heart pounds more quickly and loudly than the relaxed one.

And so in similar vein we read that 'A glad heart makes a cheerful countenance, but by sorrow of heart the spirit is broken' (Prov. 15:13). There are some people who go through life seeming much happier than others and this is not simply due to external circumstances. Some people easily see problems and are more serious by nature, while others see the funny side of life or just have a more cheerful disposition. When we are happy it shows on our faces, but a heavy heart seems to drag the whole of our bodies down – our shoulders droop, our energy dissipates, our faces hang down in sympathy. The wise too made the intrinsic connection between our inner disposition and outward expression – our mood shows in our countenance, voice and demeanour, however hard we try to cover it up! There is a similar contrast in Proverbs 17:22: 'A cheerful heart is a good medicine, but a downcast spirit dries up the bones', which conveys even more strongly the physical sensations of happiness and sadness and the realization by the wise that we are a psychosomatic unity. We are told that the best antidote to stress and anxiety is laughter. We don't normally think of bones being affected by a person's emotional state but this is a metaphor which speaks of the unity of the whole body. It is true that people who have sad lives or a sad countenance often age more quickly than those of a cheerful disposition. It is as if life's hardships have sucked the energy out of their bodies.

This contrast between happiness and sadness is found again in Proverbs 27:9: 'Oil and perfume make the heart glad, but the soul is torn by trouble.' The rather small and trivial pleasures that can cheer us up, such as pampering ourselves with aromatic oils and scents, are contrasted with the enormous and heart-rending problems that can weigh us down. Maybe we spend too much time dwelling on problems? This proverb is fraught with translation difficulties and some read the second half of the proverb not as an alternative to the gladness oil and perfume can bring but as a reference to the pleasure of friendship which strengthens the soul. This is also true, although the effects of cosmetics might be seen as rather less significant than the effects of true friendship! We read in Proverbs 14:10 that 'The heart knows its own bitterness, and no stranger shares its joy.' Only you yourself know exactly how you feel about something and ultimately no one else can fully know your sorrow or your joy. There is a private side to each of us and a set of deeper feelings which cannot be fully communicated to others. Strangers will not be pleased by your success because they do not know you – presumably the converse is that they would be unlikely to be there for you in your sorrow either. This is where friends come in – but even they are not able to share all your emotions and feelings.

There are other proverbs on the same theme which do not involve a contrast. We read, for example, in Proverbs 14:13 that 'Even in laughter the heart is sad, and the end of joy is grief.' The suggestion here that there is often sadness behind the mask of happiness and that grief is mixed with joy, resonates very much with our human experience. We may find ourselves experiencing joy and sadness simultaneously and sometimes our emotions change rapidly from one extreme to another. This proverb also suggests that outward demeanour is not always the whole story – some people are quite good at concealing their true emotions. Proverbs 25:20 uses three unusual images to make its point: 'He who sings songs to a heavy heart is like one who takes off a garment on a cold day and like vinegar on a wound.' Singing cheerful songs is anathema to an unhappy heart, while taking off clothes on a cold day is eccentric behaviour, and putting vinegar on a wound is painful. The sages were adept at drawing comparisons between unlike things and seeing what truth was contained in the analogy. Of course it is true that many of the best love songs have been written whilst their composers were in the depths of despair. This proverb may be referring to a sorrowful person having to sing cheery songs, as a job perhaps, or a person trying to cheer up someone who is depressed by singing cheerful songs. Either way the cheerfulness does not work: gaiety in the presence of sorrow is usually most unhelpful. This is a different point to cheering someone up by a well-placed word and underlines the need for discretionary and measured behaviour in trying to deal with someone who is unhappy or depressed.

We all need to have hope that something better is around the corner. A more cheerful proverb is Proverbs 15:30: 'The light of the eyes rejoices the heart, and good news refreshes the bones.' It is often said that our eyes are the windows to our souls. When we meet someone brimming with joy and enthusiasm it is bound to rub off on us and good news likewise is a great 'pick-me-up'. A friendly look from another person or shining eyes are a great tonic and good news revitalizes us: both verbal and non-verbal communication can be effective. There is a lighter side to life after all!

One of the keys to human happiness is desire fulfilled, and a few proverbs focus on this theme. We all have desires and expectations and when they are fulfilled it is a source of great joy. However, when they remain unfulfilled, our disappointment leads to grief. Proverbs 13:12 reads: 'Hope deferred makes the heart sick, but a desire fulfilled is a tree of life.' The people or situations in whom or in which we place great hope do not always live up to our expectations. Many people spend their lives putting their hopes off to another day and it is very easy to be so caught up in the daily round of tasks that we forget what we are hoping for in the long term. This proverb then expresses the discouragement and frustration that we feel when we don't achieve our aim – our energy is sapped. When a desire is fulfilled, however, it is a great moment which often has ramifications for our whole future lives. Like a tree that blossoms and grows, it is life-giving, energy-giving and fulfilling. The wise knew the satisfaction of the fulfilment of a long-held dream. We read in Proverbs 13:19: 'A desire fulfilled is sweet to the soul; but to turn away from evil is an abomination to fools.' This proverb seems to contrast two rather unlike situations: fools bent on the path of evil are compared to the sweetness of fulfilled desire. It is making the point that it is not only what fortune puts in our path that affects our destiny but how we handle what is offered. We have a choice between rejoicing in the good things of life or being weighed down and troubled by the bad. We are all bound to experience both at times, but it is how we deal with them that is the essential key to our own well-being and ultimately to the well-being of others.

There is nothing worse than seeing someone who has been broken by life. We read in Proverbs 18:14: 'A man's spirit will endure sickness; but a broken spirit who can bear?' A person suffering a physical illness can often over-come it if he or she has the will, strength and determination to do so. But people can die of a broken heart or other psychologically and emotionally related factors, as well as of actual illness. A broken spirit is much harder to mend than anything else – pills and potions will not help. Some people can overcome personal tragedy, but it is not always possible. Someone whose spirit is crushed or depressed has no zest for the warfare of life. Only the individual him or herself can ultimately make a decision to live rather than to die. The choice of life or death is in our own hands.

3

Good relationships with others

Communication and the power of words

'If I had words . . .' (*Babe*)

Words have great power: they have the power to persuade, to entice, to instruct, to educate, to woo and to cherish. The power of this fundamental tool of human communication was a source of fascination to the wise, and they used the whole range of images, including the mouth, tongue and lips, to speak about not only a person's words but his or her deeds. To the wise, words revealed an entire personality. There are numerous short and longer sayings on all aspects of this theme.

The wise preferred openness to concealment and honesty to lies. And so we read:

> He who conceals hatred has lying lips,
> and he who utters slander is a fool.
> When words are many, transgression is not
> lacking,
> but he who restrains his lips is prudent.
> The tongue of the righteous is choice silver;
> the mind of the wicked is of little worth.
> The lips of the righteous feed many,
> but fools die for lack of sense.
>
> (Prov. 10:18–21)

Here we have a series of proverbs in one passage about words. It starts with the negative ways in which speech can be used, to conceal hatred and to utter slander. The fool has a kind of cleverness that is fed by malevolence. He harbours hatred and lets it fester, an activity which is both self-destructive and destructive of others. There is a contrast in this proverb between the 'concealing' that is lying and deceit and the 'revealing' nature of slander when directed at others. Both are equally destructive in the long term.

This section goes on to treat a favourite theme of the Wisdom writers, namely the importance of restraint in speech. The wise were not in favour of gossips or those with babbling tongues. While too much talking is regarded as a sign of a fool, well-chosen words are another matter – when the righteous speak it is worth hearing, but the thoughts of fools are of no value. Normally abundance is good and scarcity is bad, but with words the opposite is true – too many words are a bad thing and many fewer (even silence) are much more preferable! In the final verse of this section, the words of the righteous are seen as an inspiration to others: thoughtful pragmatic words and deeds nurture community life as well as those who speak them. The antithesis is the path to death. Fools fail to preserve even their own lives, let alone the lives of others.

The wise make use of all the parts of the body associated with the speaking process, as Proverbs 10:31–2 illustrates: 'The mouth of the righteous brings forth wisdom, but the perverse tongue will be cut off. The lips of the righteous know what is acceptable, but the mouth of the wicked, what is perverse.' Here again the importance of the words of the righteous is contrasted with the perversions of the wicked. Good words are like a tree that is nourished: its branches grow and spread and the tree bears fruit. Bad words are equivalent to cutting the tree down. The results of both wise and foolish speech are thus clearly evident. Righteous people know how to choose their words and know what is acceptable to all, but the wicked perpetuate disruptive and destructive speech which has bad effects on others. The same point is confirmed in another proverb: 'With his mouth the godless man would destroy his neighbour, but by knowledge the righteous are delivered' (Prov. 11:9). The wise realize the power of words and the way they can be used to influence others for good or ill. Some relish speaking in a way that will bring others down. But wisdom and general acquaintance with life enables a righteous person to see through the designs of the wicked and thwart them.

The wise weighed up the impact that people's communication would have on the whole community. Good or bad speech did not simply have consequences for the individual but affected social relations and ultimately the entire social order and in turn the divine order.

> By the blessing of the upright a city is
>   exalted,
>   but it is overthrown by the mouth of the
>   wicked.
> He who belittles his neighbour lacks sense,
>   but a man of understanding remains
>   silent.
> He who goes about as a talebearer reveals
>   secrets,
>   but he who is trustworthy in spirit keeps
>   a thing hidden.
>   (Prov. 11:11–13)

Such is the positive power of words that a whole community benefits from good ones, while the negative words of the wicked can even lead to a whole city being overthrown. Control of one's speech is essential. On a personal level, too, belittling others by gossip or sheer animosity never got anyone anywhere. Those who perpetuate this are

presumably misguided enough to think that their reputa-
tions could be advanced or prospects improved by such
disloyalty, but they are wrong. Those who denigrate others
and break confidences, say the wise, are simply exposing
their own intellectual deficiencies and lack of judgement.
Silence is seen as a virtue and as a sign of a person of
discernment and understanding. Gossip is the acid test –
telling tales is a sign of an unreliable person who cannot be
trusted with secrets. The trustworthy on the other hand
will not divulge the secrets confided to them. The wise are
recommending the more difficult route – it is easy just to
tell a secret to one other person to take it off one's own
mind, but it is better not to, and so remain a person of
integrity.

Words, say the wise, can be used to entrap and deceive:
'The words of the wicked lie in wait for blood, but the
mouth of the upright delivers men' (Prov. 12:6). Here
the language becomes more intense, with the words of the
wicked being seen as traps or ambushes, waiting to catch
the unsuspecting passer-by. Escape from attack is to be
found in carefully chosen words. This may refer to the
ability of the wise to secure justice in court by the use of
effective argument. Just speech has a healing power of its
own. Proverbs 12:14 expresses the slightly different sentiment that speaking well is satisfying and repays the speaker
in the same way that hard work is never wasted: 'From the
fruit of his words a man is satisfied with good, and the work
of a man's hand comes back to him.' Words and acts
produce results for a person, i.e. one sows what one reaps.
A similar proverb is Proverbs 13:2–3: 'From the fruit of his
mouth a good man eats good, but the desire of the treach-
erous is for violence. He who guards his mouth preserves
his life; he who opens wide his lips comes to ruin.' This
reminds me of an image of the Canaanite god of death,
Mot, who is described as having a gaping mouth with which
he swallows captives whole – not a nice fate! The guarding

of one's mouth refers to the wise tendency not to speak unless one has something worthwhile to say, but to exercise some self-control; whilst its opposite is the wide open mouth that cannot stop talking and, in the removing of all restraints, is bound to offend. In contrast to the external food which one normally eats, here one metaphorically eats good, i.e. the quality of words matters and feeds the internal spirit as well as being socially fruitful.

Words of truth are a delight to hear but falsehood conversely unleashes a destructive power. And so we read:

> He who speaks the truth gives honest
>   evidence,
> but a false witness utters deceit.
> There is one whose rash words are like
>   sword thrusts,
> but the tongue of the wise brings healing.
> Truthful lips endure for ever,
> but a lying tongue is but for a moment.
>   (Prov. 12:17–19)

This series of proverbs is interesting in that truth and falsehood are perceived in terms of words being uttered. The first uses the language of the law court and praises the giving of true evidence as against false witness. Honest witness assists the process of justice whereas falsity just hinders it. The second speaks of rash words which have an immediate and negative effect and, like sword thrusts, are designed to hurt and wound others. The tongue of the wise person on the other hand has the power to effect long-term healing. Constructive words which cement human relationships are not only therapeutic to individuals but there is a community aspect that makes them healing for all, a point which is repeated in the third proverb. The power of good is more long lasting than the power of evil. Truthfulness endures and is reliable, but lies are ephemeral,

both quickly spoken and quickly forgotten. There are over-
tones here of the immediacy of the lie, often uttered before
it is even properly thought through and so open to discovery. God hates lying: 'Lying lips are an abomination to
the Lord, but those who act faithfully are his delight' (Prov.
12:22). This is a strong condemnation of speech perverted
from its normal function. Lying furthermore becomes a
habit: 'A faithful witness does not lie, but a false witness
breathes out lies' (Prov. 14:5) – again a reference to perjury
in the law court – and 'A truthful witness saves lives, but
one who utters lies is a betrayer' (Prov. 14:25). Honesty in
such a situation could save the life of an innocent defendant
who might otherwise be sent to the gallows. The one who
utters lies obscures the truth of a case and so could lead to
the wrong decision being taken. These proverbs show
clearly the social aspect of truth and falsehood.

The wise also understood that two keys of successful
communication are about when and how something is said:
'A soft answer turns away wrath, but a harsh word stirs up
anger. The tongue of the wise dispenses knowledge, but the
mouths of fools pour out folly' (Prov. 15:1–2). A gentle
and tactful answer is clearly so much better than a remark
snapped back without thought which just causes offence. In
saying this the wise are not advocating appeasement at any
cost, but a studied conciliatory approach with the use of
effective words. The power of the spoken word to rouse to
anger is also recognized – an inflammatory situation is very
quickly created but much harder to dispel. Wise people
who speak carefully and eloquently are worth listening to,
whereas babbling fools are not. In the same vein, 'A gentle
tongue is a tree of life, but perverseness in it breaks the
spirit' (Prov. 15:4). Words kindly and diplomatically
spoken are so much better than deliberately cutting words
which break the spirit of others. Words have real effect and
are either therapeutic or destructive. In fact, there can
never be too many kind words as they are a source of

vitality to others. Also, remembering to speak up when it is deserved is important: 'To make an apt answer is a joy to a man, and a word in season, how good it is!' (Prov. 15:23). Good advice has to be accompanied by good timing; it is counter-productive having pertinent things to say but getting the timing wrong. Communicating well and effectively is not just a pleasure to the person who is speaking but everyone benefits. Good conversation is itself an art and a joy.

A proverb that also relates to planning (see pp. 56–65) mentions the God-given nature of the right answer: 'The plans of the mind belong to man, but the answer of the tongue is from the Lord' (Prov. 16:1). Planning and speaking wisely are closely related – the well thought-out reply is usually more beneficial than the unplanned word, especially when rational thought rather than an angry response is needed. But human beings should never forget that they are ultimately dependent on God for the successful outcome of plans – humans may think many thoughts but the ability to speak the right answer is seen to come from God. We see here the tension mentioned earlier between free will and the purposes of God. Furthermore, a well thought-out answer is generally more persuasive than a rushed one: 'The mind of the wise makes his speech judicious, and adds persuasiveness to his lips. Pleasant words are like a honeycomb, sweetness to the soul and health to the body' (Prov. 16:23–4). Those who are wise think before they speak, thus ensuring that their words are effective: they argue their case so that they can successfully persuade. Eloquence and perhaps a spot of charm are seen as sweet and medicinal. On the other hand, 'A worthless man plots evil, and his speech is like a scorching fire. A perverse man spreads strife, and a whisperer separates close friends' (Prov. 16:27–8). Deep-seated malevolence leads to enmity, prompting words that are like fire: they are hot and unpleasant and spread like wildfire. The person who tells tales can cause immense harm in society, even deliberately trying to separate friends by inciting discord and endeavouring to break down mutual trust.

Restraint in words is usually advocated, but there is a double edge to this because anyone who keeps silent can be considered wise when in fact they are not: 'He who restrains his words has knowledge, and he who has a cool spirit is a man of understanding. Even a fool who keeps silent is considered wise; when he closes his lips, he is deemed intelligent' (Prov. 17:27–8). In verse 27 economy of utterance is commended along with self-mastery, moderation and restraint which is characterized here as 'coolness'. This is in contrast to those who become heated in their speech or who are hot-headed. However, verse 28 makes the point that, ironically, fools might appear wise when they are silent, but the probable truth of the matter is that they find it extremely hard to keep quiet and are usually betrayed by their loquaciousness! The wise thought it always better to say as little as possible and only to speak when one had something worthwhile to say, thus avoiding the danger of making a fool of oneself. It is against the order of things that fools should speak well: 'Fine speech is not becoming to a fool; still less is false speech to a prince' (Prov. 17:7). Those in authority ought to know better than to tell lies to those in their charge, and yet how often this happens. Behaviour that is out of character on either side causes confusion, but the wise were more appalled by lying by one of rank than even by the babbling of fools.

Be careful to whom you listen, warn the wise! 'An evildoer listens to wicked lips; and a liar gives heed to a mischievous tongue' (Prov. 17:4). People tend to listen to what they want to hear. Malevolent people listen to malicious gossip in order to harm others, to promote faction and ill-will. They pass on falsity as truth and other people enjoy the gossip. Words are very powerful, revealing the profundity of the inner self: 'The words of a man's mouth are deep waters; the fountain of wisdom is a gushing stream' (Prov. 18:4). Deep waters suggest the inner self which is brought to the surface as a fountain of wisdom that can be shared with others. There is also the overtone that wisdom, like a fountain, is a source of refreshment, and, like a fountain which never runs out of flowing water, wise words are never lacking.

All speech has consequences. Words can be very satisfying and lead along the path to life but they can also be used to lead to destruction and death: 'From the fruit of his mouth a man is satisfied; he is satisfied by the yield of his lips. Death and life are in the power of the tongue, and those who love it will eat its fruits' (Prov. 18:20–1). Like a harvest, words can bear fruit for the individual and society. People will experience either life or death depending on the quality of their words. Even if their intentions were not evil, fools also suffer the consequences of their actions when their mouths run away with them: 'A fool's lips bring strife, and his mouth invites a flogging. A fool's mouth is his ruin, and his lips are a snare to himself. The words of a whisperer are like delicious morsels; they go down into the inner parts of the body' (Prov. 18:6–8). Slander is particularly dangerous: people listen to it avidly, remembering it and allowing it to affect their thoughts and actions.

The look on a person's face or his or her manner usually reveals when there has been strife: 'The north wind brings forth rain; and a backbiting tongue, angry looks' (Prov. 25:23). Just as a particular wind brings an unexpected downpour of rain, so the tongue that speaks ill of people behind their backs generates angry looks, presumably on the part of those who are being gossiped about. Slander stirs up anger – and we know how the wise despised that! Nearly as bad is gossip: 'He who goes about gossiping reveals secrets; therefore do not associate with one who speaks foolishly' (Prov. 20:19). If you value your privacy, avoid gossips! We are given a picture again of a weak, inquisitive, troublesome person who cannot keep a secret, in stark contrast to the person who can control his or her speech and keep a confidence. Such a person 'keeps his mouth and his tongue keeps himself out of trouble' (Prov. 21:23).

Lying is not recommended. Truth will out. 'A false witness will not go unpunished, and he who utters lies will not escape' (Prov. 19:5), and in similar vein, 'A false witness will not go unpunished, and he who utters lies will perish' (Prov. 19:9). Perjury was a serious crime that had to be punished (cf. Prov. 6:19; 12:17; 14:5, 25; 21:28). Lying is equally dangerous when it is used to get rich, as we saw in connection with the proverbs on money: 'The getting of treasures by a lying tongue is a fleeting vapour and a snare of death' (Prov. 21:6). Any apparent success from lying is fleeting and in the long term is a trap.

There is virtue in keeping oneself to oneself, in controlling one's speech and even being taciturn at times. The wise advocate a quiet life: 'Drive out a scoffer, and strife will go out, and quarrelling and abuse will cease' (Prov. 22:10). The community has a responsibility to rid itself of insolent, argumentative types who destroy others and stir up strife. Such troublemakers should be driven out of the public assembly. On the other hand, 'A word fitly spoken is like apples of gold in a setting of silver' (Prov. 25:11). Words spoken in appropriate situations have immense value. They are likened to the golden apples inside a silver case or carving, which would constitute the most valuable part of the object. In fact, the power of persuasion can be very strong, even when dealing with a ruler, although on such occasions especial care is needed: 'With patience a ruler may be persuaded, and a soft tongue will break a bone' (Prov. 25:15). Persuasiveness is perceived as better than confrontation any day. However, don't go overboard: 'It is not good to eat much honey, so be sparing of complimentary words' (Prov. 25:27). Although there are difficulties in the translation of this proverb, it is clear that it is promoting moderation in all things.

Other aspects of communicating are also discussed, such as impulsive speech that leads to not listening to others: 'If one gives answer before he hears, it is his folly and shame' (Prov. 18:13). This is another sign of being undisciplined and self-opinionated, which will just reveal a person's true foolish nature and lead to humiliation. It was important to the wise to listen to others so that true dialogue could take place. Self-praise is also not recommended: 'Let another praise you, and not your own mouth; a stranger, and not your own lips' (Prov. 27:2). Self-praise does not have anything like the same significance as the praise of others and in fact too much self-advertisement could have the opposite effect of ruining a person's reputation. The judgement of a stranger might be said to be unbiased, but as the stranger does not know the person he or she is talking about, perhaps the praise of an honest friend is better.

Hasty speech was also considered as very unwise: 'Do you see a man who is hasty in his words? There is more hope for a fool than for him' (Prov. 29:20). Here again we have the theme of lack of control of words which can lead to rash and ill considered speech or action. The wise recommend the occasional word of rebuke when disciplining someone rather than flattery which they cannot abide: 'He who rebukes a man will afterward find more favour than he who flatters with his tongue' (Prov. 28:23). It is perhaps necessary to be 'cruel to be kind'. A rebuke may not be very welcome, but if it is honest a person will often come to see that it was helpful. Flattery on the other hand is easily heard but not lasting or real. The wise call for honesty believing that a candid opinion is better than a barrage of false flattery.

A long diatribe in Proverbs 26:20–28 reiterates some of the themes with which we are now familiar:

For lack of wood the fire goes out;
>   and where there is no whisperer,
>   quarrelling ceases.
As charcoal to hot embers and wood to fire,
>   so is a quarrelsome man for kindling
>   strife.
The words of a whisperer are like delicious
>   morsels;
>   they go down into the inner parts of the
>   body.
Like the glaze covering an earthen vessel
>   are smooth lips with an evil heart.
He who hates, dissembles with his lips
>   and harbours deceit in his heart;
when he speaks graciously, believe him not,
>   for there are seven abominations in his
>   heart;
though his hatred be covered with guile,
>   his wickedness will be exposed in the
>   assembly.
He who digs a pit will fall into it,
>   and a stone will come back upon him who
>   starts it rolling.
A lying tongue hates its victims,
>   and a flattering mouth works ruin.

Gossip, often instigated by troublesome people who purposely fan the flames of dissension, causes quarrelling. When the gossip stops, the fire goes out, but unfortunately by then the damage has been done and some people inevitably take the damaging talk on board (v.22, in a repeat of Prov. 18:8). Like a glaze that makes a pot look valuable and attractive when it is in fact, worthless, everything may look all very pleasant on the surface when in reality the intention it is covering up is evil. All too often malice is cloaked by charm and gracious speaking. Although the troublemaker loves to conceal his hatred, the message of the wise is that in the end society will see through him and the truth will out. Then he will be hoisted by his own petard. Hatred and lying, which often go together, have the effect of crushing others, and, along with flattery, lead to their ruin. However, they often rebound on the liar himself.

Gossip or idle chatter can be likened to the game of Chinese whispers which can either run out of steam or can gain momentum so that the original words get more and more distorted. The fire of strife is fuelled by rumours and quarrelsomeness – but, ask the wise, what is the point of quarrelling with everyone? Proverbs 3:30 urges, 'Do not contend with a man for no reason, when he has done you no harm', but it seems that there are some people who are all too ready to pick a quarrel without good cause. The wise are cautious both of smooth talkers and those who appear friendly on the surface but are in fact deceitful. They believed that such people would eventually be exposed and their deeds come back to haunt them.

So the importance of choosing one's words carefully, of thinking through what one wants to say, of speaking concisely and not too often, of restraining oneself from gossiping and spreading secrets is emphasized over and over again by the wise. There are plenty of warnings against evil, hasty, or foolish words and the bad consequences that will inevitably ensue. Words exert great power, and so their use and abuse is of prime importance. These reflections of the wise may lead us to consider how we use or abuse words. Do we always think carefully before we speak? Do we sometimes use words deliberately to hurt and wound? Do we use words of tenderness and love enough in our busy lives? Do we gossip and babble too much, or, conversely, do we sometimes fail to speak out on important matters?

Authority

A cat may look on a King. (John Heywood)

Although the hierarchical world of kings, masters and servants no longer has the relevance today that it once had, we
all face issues of authority in our lives. The authority our
parents have over us when we are young gradually lessens as
we reach adolescence and need to make our own decisions
and choices. In the work situation we are answerable to our
peers and to those who are senior to us. In our many
relationships there are different dependency patterns so
that whereas in one relationship or set of relationships a
person may carry more authority, in another he or she may
be the one who is subject. A good deal of this has to do
with personality − some people are natural leaders while
others are happier to follow the lead given to them. The
Wisdom writers were concerned to link authority and
wisdom. They realized the power of those in authority
and were keen to ensure that such power should not be
misused. They also understood how those who might seem
subservient could sometimes scheme their way to higher
positions by turning the heads of those in authority.

We begin with proverbs about masters and servants. In
the view of the wise, a figure of authority who abuses the
trust that his household put in him will not reap the benefits
of a happy household. The key to successful leadership is
fair dealing and good treatment of those under your power:
'He who troubles his household will inherit wind, and the
fool will be servant to the wise' (Prov. 11:29). This proverb
probably refers to bad management of family resources on
the part of the head of the family. He only has himself to
blame for injuring his economic situation through negli-
gence or incapacity and at the end of the day he will lose
both his personal liberty and inheritance because he cannot
manage his own household.

Servants are also expected to behave well since otherwise they will incur the wrath of those in authority over them. So we read that 'A servant who deals wisely has the king's favour, but his wrath falls on one who acts shamefully' (Prov. 14:35). The king is of course the ultimate 'leader' but this maxim can be translated into any situation of subservience. If you do not deal wisely in your job, for example, you are likely to incur the wrath of your boss! It is up to the leader of any group to choose advisers carefully and anyone who acts skilfully in administrative affairs, whatever his or her status, has a chance of making it to the top.

Returning to the theme of words and communication, good communication is essential to a master/servant relationship. Those in authority need to convey their expectations to those who serve them. This sometimes involves the need for discipline if, for example, a servant becomes too bold and starts to ignore what the master is saying: 'By mere words a servant is not disciplined, for though he understands, he will not give heed' (Prov. 29:19). Although at first this proverb seems to be condoning physical discipline over a verbal reprimand, suggesting that only corporal punishment will cure the kind of insolence that makes someone unteachable, there is more to it than that. It is a duty on the part of the master to lead by example. Often those in control are keen to delegate but wouldn't be seen dead doing the task themselves! Aren't the most successful managers those who have been on the shop floor and done the difficult tasks themselves? The proverb paints the scene of a servant who hears but does not take any notice – there is no proper dialogue between master and servant. Perhaps the master has said the words once too often, or maybe he has lost the respect of his servant.

Still on the subject of words, another proverb deals with the whole topic of gossip and backbiting in relation to masters and servants: 'Do not slander a servant to his master, lest he curse you, and you be held guilty' (Prov.

30:10). Although this proverb applies specifically to those in positions of power, it is a general truth that criticizing someone in the hearing of another is a risky practice, which may rebound upon the speaker. The criticism may get back to the person concerned who may then harbour a grudge, even if, perhaps, the culprit was merely repeating someone else's criticism. It is generally unwise to pass on gossip even if it is true – better to mind one's own business and not get involved in the affairs of other people. With regard to the situation specifically mentioned in the proverb, a person who criticizes a servant to his master's face, may himself or herself end up facing misery. The master is likely to be loyal to his own household and take any slight against his servant as a slight against himself, or it may even be the servant himself who curses his attacker – either way the meddler will be found out!

Others proverbs in this category speak of the importance wisdom plays in enabling a person to get to the top. A wise slave may even conquer over a misbehaving son: 'A slave who deals wisely will rule over a son who acts shamefully, and will share the inheritance as one of the brothers' (Prov. 17:2). The wise are stressing here that family bonds are not enough to secure an inheritance without being accompanied by good behaviour. It is a warning to sons not to shirk their duties. How often have people lost their inheritance through unwise actions! Good behaviour and wisdom are fountains of life and a slave who understands this will go far. Wisdom can transcend natural boundaries and expecta-tions. However, there is a cautionary note in that a servant upon whom a master relies too much, may take advantage of the situation. A family may be cheated out of their inheritance by the wiles of a friend or neighbour who, often in the case of elderly people, have found their way into the older person's affections, become dependable and reliable, and as a result been favoured in a will or legacy. When the family discover that they have been displaced by a person they perceive as an outsider, mayhem can ensue.

Servants have to be kept in their place. So we read that 'He who pampers his servant from childhood, will in the end find him his heir' (Prov. 29:21). According to the wise it is not good to overindulge someone who is under your authority – it is better to maintain some distance for otherwise that person will take advantage and manoeuvre himself or herself into a position in which he or she inherits all that you have. The translation of the second part of this proverb is uncertain, but it is clear that pampering a slave is not going to achieve anything but difficulty for the master. Proverbs 30:21–3 mentions the possibility of a slave becoming king – the ultimate in the least becoming first! Note that the Wisdom writers do not think that this is a good thing and there is a certain humour in the way they, again using the device of numbers, present such inversion of the social order as a cosmic-type upheaval: 'Under three things the earth trembles; under four it cannot bear up: a slave when he becomes king, and a fool when he is filled with food; an unloved woman when she gets a husband, and a maid when she succeeds her mistress.' These are unnatural occurrences that are against the order that is society and which is upheld by God. The fool should not have enough to eat because that depends on virtuous and responsible behaviour, of which he has none! An unloved woman – perhaps because she is unattractive or a spinster – is unlikely to find a husband but fortunately for her, and surprisingly in the societal order, she does. And a maid supplanting her mistress is bound to cause trouble! The Wisdom writers are not just commenting on the change of social position that all these situations have in common but also on the behaviour of those whose fortunes do change – they could all become rather unbearable to live with!

Next, we move on to kings and rulers specifically. Again, in a world where few kings and queens have real political power, we could perhaps apply these maxims to anyone in authority, whether it be in the wider world of politicians and presidents or in the narrower world of any of the leaders in our own corners of society. There is a recognition amongst the Wisdom writers that, since there are clearly good kings and bad kings, leadership can on the one hand be a great gift and strength and worthy of infinite respect but, on the other, its abuse leads to great problems and inequalities. There are a number of proverbs that urge obedience towards the king and that warn of the dangers of angering him. After all, he has the power to destroy those with whom he is displeased, whether he is justified in doing so or not. Kings are at the top of the preferment tree – rouse the king's anger and you are in severe danger. With any ruler there is a great danger of either being 'in' or 'out' of favour. One thinks perhaps of politicians who are at one moment at the height of their power and command the respect of their peers but who are then discredited, forced to resign and become *persona non grata*. In Proverbs 20:2 we read that 'the dread wrath of a king is like the growling of a lion; he who provokes him to anger forfeits his life' (cf. Prov. 19:12). As the king of the forest and one of the fiercest creatures known on earth and famous for the loudness and ferocity of its roar, the lion is a pertinent image for a king. The power of the king spells danger for unpopular subjects. He must be treated with extreme care!

The wise also draw comparisons between respecting the king and respecting God. As God's representative on earth the king was regarded as worthy of respect: 'My son, fear the Lord and the king, and do not disobey either of them; for disaster from them will rise suddenly, and who knows the ruin that will come from them both?' (Prov. 24:21–2). The price of disobedience is high in a society that believes firmly in the merits of doing right and the punishments that wrongdoing will incur. The advice here is to keep a low profile – avoid intrigue or dissident behaviour which could be the cause of both divine and human wrath. The wise, as we have already seen, tended to phrase their advice in a rather black and white way!

However, there is also a recognition of the differences between God and king. While God knows all things – although at times he may choose to hide his secrets – kings – although they at times may also be inscrutable – lead the human quest for understanding and need to know what is going on. So we read:

> It is the glory of God to conceal things,
>> but the glory of kings is to search things out.
> As the heavens for height, and the earth for depth,
>> so the mind of kings is unsearchable.
> Take away the dross from the silver,
>> and the smith has material for a vessel;
> take away the wicked from the presence of the king,
>> and his throne will be established in righteousness.
> Do not put yourself forward in the king's presence
>> or stand in the place of the great;
> for it is better to be told, "Come up here,"
>> than to be put lower in the presence of the prince.
>
> (Prov. 25:2–7)

In their use of the image of the smelting process which purifies metal so that it can be used to make a fitting vessel, the wise were expressing their disgust for the wicked who pollute purity. Kings are surrounded by counsellors who are notoriously often less than pure in their motives for being there and anxious to line their own nests. Their invidious influence on the king is best removed in order to ensure righteous rule. The wise also warned against being too pushy: they were great believers in humility and in genuine reward for humble service as against favour for those who pushed themselves forward. It is better to wait for another to call you, rather than promote yourself. Modesty has its own reward. This is very practical advice for our society today in which pushing oneself forward and trying to be noticed often pays off. However, even today, we are wary of brash self-seeking rather than genuine merit. The line is a hard one to draw and it is particularly difficult for those who are young and seeking to get on. Is it better to push and use all the connections we have or to take a humble back seat aiming to get on by our own merits alone, hoping perhaps that someone will notice our worth without our having to proclaim it to the world?

Good communication also plays its part in our relation-ships with those in authority. We read that,

> Righteous lips are the delight of a king
>   and he loves him who speaks what is
>   right.
> A king's wrath is a messenger of death,
>   and a wise man will appease it.
> In the light of a king's face there is life,
>   and his favour is like the clouds that bring
>   the spring rain.
>   (Prov. 16:13–15)

The second two proverbs in this sequence recall ones con-sidered above: faced with the king's wrath anyone with any sense will try to calm him down and make him see his or her own side of the argument. Heat and anger are the enemies of wisdom which promotes self-control and candid dialogue. By contrast the favour of the king is a great privilege and to be sought at all times. Again the image of refreshing rain is used, something that is not under human control. Careers are made or broken by the leaders of society. Saying the right word at the right time is crucial. The king needs to be surrounded by wise counsellors not by drivelling fools. Those in the monarch's service, who perhaps see him every day, probably feel that they are in his trust, but there is always the danger that power will go to their head and that they will become accustomed, for example, to the fine banquets and special treatment they receive. Such people must beware of over-reaching themselves: 'When you sit down to eat with a ruler, observe carefully what is before you; and put a knife to your throat if you are a man given to appetite. Do not desire his delicacies, for they are deceptive food' (Prov. 23:1–3). This proverb cleverly uses the imagery of food and eating to make its point – good food in moderation is one thing, gluttony is another! As well as its obvious interpretation as advice on eating at table, it can be read as referring to advancing in one's career. When you sit down with a leader with the aim of currying favour, observe your host carefully and restrain yourself by not over-indulging. That would be rather like getting drunk with the boss when you are trying to impress him! In the frame of reference of the proverb, avarice will be noted by the host who is perhaps using this opportunity as a test of character.

Good kings are a great joy: 'If a king judges the poor with equity his throne will be established for ever' (Prov. 29:14). The wise were especially concerned that the poor, who were less secure and in a weaker position, should receive justice. This was the special duty of the king and in fact this proverb sees the duration of a dynasty as depending on his moral character in this regard. But bad kings are all too prevalent. On some occasions overindulgence can lead to injustice being perpetuated, and inebriation is the enemy of royal justice: 'It is not for kings, O Lemuel, it is not for kings to drink wine, or for rulers to desire strong drink; lest they drink and forget what has been decreed, and pervert the rights of all the afflicted' (Prov. 31:4–5). This is a warning against the danger of overindulgence in drink for a ruler must always be in a fit state to make the right decisions. A wicked king is a terrible thing and the misuse of power in any situation is frightening: 'Like a roaring lion or a charging bear is a wicked ruler over a poor people. A ruler who lacks understanding is a cruel oppressor; but he who hates unjust gain will prolong his days' (Prov. 28:15–16). In the last century there have been many examples of the misuse of power by leaders, Hitler being perhaps the prime example. It is interesting that longevity is again associated with wise rule. A king must uphold what is right and oppose criminal behaviour and crooked dealings. If the person in charge is corrupt it tends to filter down into the organization, as this proverb suggests: 'If a ruler listens to falsehood, all his officials will be wicked' (Prov. 29:12).

It is a hard job being a ruler and in the public eye all the time. Whether a king or queen, or a person in any type of authority, all of his or her deeds are analysed and scrutinized by others and one foot wrong can undo a lifetime of good deeds. On the other hand it is hard for power not to go to a person's head and for leaders to ensure that they are surrounding themselves with the right people.

Family relationships

A child should always say what's true
And speak when he is spoken to
And behave mannerly at table
At least as far as he is able.

(Robert Louis Stevenson)

The family unit is at the heart of human life and society. We were all born into a family, although some may sadly have been separated from it. As well as the close family of parents and siblings, there is the wider family of grand-parents, uncles, aunts and cousins with whom we are genetically related and may share similarities in both looks and temperament. We do not choose our family in the way that we choose our friends, and relationships within families can be the best or the worst that we ever experience. As such a key area of human experience it was bound to preoccupy the wise. Many proverbial sayings may have orig-inated in the family and, as sources of truth and guidance, may have been passed down through the gen-erations as the fruits of collected experience.

Perhaps the primary family relationship is that of parent and child. In the eyes of the Wisdom writers, children, like adults, have a duty to behave wisely, but some children are naturally wiser than others. We sometimes meet children who seem older and wiser than they are expected to be at a certain age. Proverbs 10:1, the opening proverb of the sayings collection, states that 'A wise son makes a glad father, but a foolish son is a sorrow to his mother.' Children often forget that their behaviour directly impacts on their parents. Parents want the best for their children and worry about their offspring's future well-being. They are often very long-suffering but at the end of the day a problematic child causes them great stress and pain, whilst a con-siderate, well-behaved child is a joy. The behaviour of children rebounds on the rest of the family, on its good name and social standing. Thus, we read in Proverbs 13:1: 'A wise son hears his father's instruction but a scoffer does not listen to rebuke.' It is the task of every parent to instruct and discipline his or her child but when their instruction is ignored by an ill-disciplined and unteachable child it can lead to difficulty. The wise believed that children should show absolute deference to their parents and should listen carefully to their wisdom. Children need to realize that, when they give them guidance in whatever sphere that may be, their parents have much more experience of life and the world and have their best interests at heart. Those who forget that and wilfully go along their own way are both misguided and foolish. One thinks particularly of teenagers who want to start to establish their independence and yet are still in the position of being essentially under their parents' authority. This is a difficult period of transition for all concerned. It is easy to scoff and to ignore wise advice, we are told – it is harder to take it on board and change one's behaviour accordingly.

A number of proverbs warn about the consequences of stupid or foolish behaviour on the part of children. As these proverbs make clear there is a difference between intellectual or moral stupidity and sheer foolishness. They do not contrast wise and foolish behaviour, they simply focus on the foolishness: 'A stupid son is a grief to a father; and the father of a fool has no joy' (Prov. 17:21). The failure of children to live up to their parents' expectations, academically or otherwise, can lead to some very difficult situations in which the parents feel let down and the child feels misunderstood and unappreciated. Good parenting realizes a child's strengths and builds upon them. However, a child who persists in behaving stupidly when he or she is not fundamentally stupid, is even more grievous to his or her parents: 'A foolish son is a grief to his father and bitterness to her who bore him' (Prov. 17:25). Here we have the recognition that both father and mother are equally affected by a child's foolish behaviour while a son or daughter doesn't always recognize the hurt he or she is causing.

There is also a close relationship between family training and family pride. Another source of concern to the parents is how other people are going to react when they see the family facing problems. The wise were very aware of the parental side of the relationship.

Proverbs 19:26–7 is a longer proverb about the erring child: 'He who does violence to his father and chases away his mother is a son who causes shame and brings reproach. Cease, my son, to hear instruction only to stray from the words of knowledge.' Sometimes children get the upper hand over their parents and use the power that they hold to do them down or mistreat them. This may happen when parents become old and infirm. This proverb is most probably describing the chasing away of elderly parents from their own house and the grasping of their inheritance by the children. Not only does this behaviour show complete lack of respect and break the commandment to honour one's parents, but it also evokes the condemnation of the rest of the community. It is the duty of the children to care for their parents when they are elderly. A child who neglects this duty is to be publicly shamed and reproached. This is an important point because, although we might think that what we do behind closed doors is a private matter, in fact our actions often have wider ramifications. When friends and supporters of the parents who are being treated in this disrespectful way hear of it, the son or daughter's reputation will be as nothing in the community.

Those who seemingly sit at the feet of the wise to learn instruction but in reality ignore it are simply wasting their own and other people's time. Wisdom must be lived out. In Proverbs 28:24, in which family property is again at stake, we read: 'He who robs his father or his mother and says, "That is no transgression" is the companion of a man who destroys.' The most worrying aspect of this manipulation on the part of the adult child is that there is a lack of shame and no sense that it is wrong! These proverbs sometimes seem so contemporary! Children can come under the influence of others – other children or adults – who make them lose their sense of right and wrong.

Parents too can be guilty of not teaching their children enough about moral distinctions. Children need to be brought up with a conscience so that they know what is right and what is wrong and so that they are equipped to make the right decisions as they attain adulthood. If they do wrong without displaying any sense of conscience about it, they have been seriously misled: they are on the road to self-destruction.

Those who lack respect for their parents are chastised again at the start of a list of different types of unnatural behaviour in Proverbs 30:11–14. In verse 11 we read: 'There are those who curse their fathers and do not bless their mothers.' We are all indebted to our parents for the gift of life itself, as well as for their love and their nurture. Even if they have not been perfect – and parenting is a hard job – the majority of us have much for which to be grateful. Proverbs 30:17 makes a similar point but adds the consequences of wrongdoing: 'The eye that mocks a father and scorns to obey a mother will be picked out by the ravens of the valley and eaten by the vultures.' Here, the scornful eye that shows contempt for parents represents the child who commits a crime against his or her parents: it is so unnatural that nature itself will carry out the punishment – the offender will die in a desolate place where his or her corpse will be eaten by ravens and vultures. In Jewish society it was and still is a real taboo to leave bodies exposed without affording them a proper burial. Of course, this needn't be taken literally! Those who go down this path of scorn will find their life going down the wrong track. Those who do ill to others, can expect the same in return.

Another group of proverbs is concerned with parental discipline which was very important to the wise men. Nowadays the majority of people do not believe in physical discipline, but prefer to rely on verbal discipline and reasoned argument. The wise, however, saw merit in a firm hand from time to time, believing it to be character forming! So we read, 'He who spares the rod hates his son, but he who loves him is diligent to discipline him' (Prov. 13:24). The point they are making is that lax parenting is not good for children. Giving in to children and giving them everything they want is a road to disaster. A firm guiding hand, instilling a moral sense, and at times a sharp word of discipline are necessary so that children learn the boundaries of acceptable behaviour. Parents who do not do this are letting their child down in the long run as well as making a rod for their own backs. It reminds me of the popular saying 'being cruel to be kind'. A child might perceive the denial of a request as a hardship at the time, but will perhaps realize later on that he or she didn't need it or want it anyway. Proverbs 19:18 tells parents to 'Discipline your son while there is hope; do not set your heart on his destruction.' Parents need to understand that discipline is a good thing, especially early training whilst there is still hope of amendment, but that too much pressure on a child is a bad thing. A child needs sometimes to be indulged or encouraged or to feel a parent's support. However, there is nothing worse than parental abuse or neglect. Even excessive chastisement is unfair on the child. A bad upbringing at the hands of misguided parents is likely to result in a child ending up on the wrong path.

The wise believed in the sound training of children: 'Train up a child in the way he should go, and when he is old he will not depart from it' (Prov. 22:6). It is said that the first five years of life are the most formative in developing an individual's personality, but it is true of childhood in general. Good habits and good sense instilled in a person during childhood become second nature. This is the responsibility of parents. It does not just happen, it has to be worked upon. Time needs to be given to the nurture and instruction of children – the younger they are the quicker they are to learn. The reference to the 'way' in which a child should go is probably to the 'right way', i.e.

the path of wisdom, but it could refer to the 'way his
aptitudes take him' in that all children have their own
strengths and weaknesses, skills and preferences, and these
need to be encouraged or discouraged by parents as appropriate. However, children should not be allowed simply to
go their own way – they all need guidance and that is the
role of the parents.

The theme of discipline is never far away. Proverbs 22:15
reads: 'Folly is bound up in the heart of a child, but the rod
of discipline drives it far from him.' Unless they are taught
it, children do not know what behaviour is appropriate.
There is a natural tendency towards folly, to use the
language of the wise, because wisdom is something learned,
something external to the human person. The educator has
the role of 'unteaching' bad habits as well as teaching good
ones! We live in a cultured society where we do not apply
the laws of the jungle to our lives and every child has to
learn to live in that society so that all its citizens can enjoy
the benefits of mutual respect and good behaviour. Thus,
some discipline is needed in every child's life to enable him
or her to learn when he or she is going astray. This doesn't
have to be phrased in terms of the 'rod': it can simply be
seen as a good practice by any parent to tell a child when he
or she has done wrong and to make it clear that such
behaviour will not be tolerated. There is a recognition here
that children are morally immature and need to be led in
the right direction. Proverbs 29:15 reinforces the same
point: 'The rod and reproof give wisdom, but a child left to
himself brings shame to his mother.' It also indicates that it
is the responsibility of the parent to train the child and that
shame will rebound upon the neglectful parent who has not
ensured that this duty has been done.

Mothers have a particular responsibility for the early
education of a child, as the admonition in Proverbs 29:17
makes clear: 'Discipline your son, and he will give you rest;
he will give delight to your heart.' A well-disciplined child

is a joy – the child is better off because he or she is secure in knowing what is expected and what the limitations are, and the parent is better off because he or she has done his or her duty and can reap the benefits of a more stress-free life as a result.

Another clear statement of the need for discipline is made finally in Proverbs 23:13–16:

> Do not withhold discipline from a child;
>> if you beat him with a rod, he will not
>>> die.
> If you beat him with the rod
>> you will save his life from Sheol.
> My son, if your heart is wise,
>> my heart too will be glad.
> My soul will rejoice
>> when your lips speak what is right.

Again, this is phrased in terms of a rod, but it can easily be translated into the more humane methods of today. A little discipline does not harm anyone and it certainly will not kill them, but an unstructured, ill-disciplined life will meta-phorically kill a child. According to the wise the path of folly and wickedness leads to death in Sheol, the place of the dead. Good parenting involves the discipline that will prevent a child taking that route. Wisdom leads to joy and pleasure on behalf of father and son – itself a strong bond – and when a father hears his son utter wise words on his own account and from his own heart he can be really proud that he has done a good job.

A kind of diatribe against every form of excess also needs to be considered in this section, since it also includes advice for parents and children:

> Hear, my son, and be wise,
>> and direct your mind in the way.
> Be not among winebibbers,

or among gluttonous eaters of meat;
for the drunkard and the glutton will come
to poverty,
and drowsiness will clothe a man with
rags.
Hearken to your father who begot you,
and do not despise your mother when she
is old.
Buy truth, and do not sell it;
buy wisdom, instruction, and
understanding.
The father of the righteous will greatly
rejoice;
he who begets a wise son will be glad in
him.
Let your father and mother be glad,
let her who bore you rejoice.
My son, give me your heart,
and let your eyes observe my ways.
For a harlot is a deep pit;
an adventuress is a narrow well;
She lies in wait like a robber
and increases the faithless among men.
(Prov. 23:19–28)

Most parents feel responsible for the way their children turn out. If they become gluttons or drunkards it is usually because there is something missing in their lives. This may be due to other factors than their upbringing but, on the other hand, there may be deep-seated weaknesses or an element of rebellion that first led to them walking down such roads to destruction as these represent. Even later in life we often have much to learn from our parents. We should not despise our parents when they become old but should still aim to make them joyful and proud to call us their children. We should avoid sexual immorality and make good choices. The 'me' in the above passage could be the wise man giving the advice or it could be wisdom personified as a woman, recalling the portrayal of Woman Wisdom in Proverbs 1–9. She calls to the young to follow her path and warns against the adulteress or adventuress (cf. Prov. 7) who lurks in the street ready to ambush the unsuspecting youngster and from whose clutches there is no escape. Since these are attractive figures that can easily lure a young man from the right path, the instruction here is to keep on the straight and narrow and remember what one has learned from one's parents.

A final short proverb speaks of the child apart from its parents: 'Even a child makes himself known by his acts, whether what he does is pure and right' (Prov. 20:11). Like it or not we are all judged by our actions which do speak louder than words, to quote another popular saying. Even as children, if we do wrong, we are condemned by others – by our elders and by our peers. How much more important it is then that we know how to behave as adults! A person's character is partly in the genes but a good deal of it is formed early in life and does not fundamentally change. Since conduct is always a test of character, training needs to begin early. We need to have a moral sense that is tuned into what is right from a young age. If we remember that, we will not go far wrong. This is all good advice from the wise. They have nothing to gain by it – it is simply borne of observation and experience.

Husbands and wives

All you need is love . . . (The Beatles)

Another primary relationship is, of course, that between husband and wife. The sages advised marriage and, along with longevity, saw children and many descendants as the sign of true blessing. They were gifts from God and ensured the continuation of the family line. In Proverbs 18:22 the wise state that 'He who finds a wife finds a good thing, and obtains favour from the Lord.' The human and divine stand side by side in this proverb – the man finds a wife but the fact that she turns out to be a good one is a divine blessing! The wise perpetuate the advice found elsewhere in Scripture that it is better to enjoy being in relationship than to be alone and that human beings should 'be fruitful and multiply' (cf. e.g. Gen. 9:1). Of course in the days of the wise, women were essentially child-bearers and looked after the home. For them there was little chance of education or an independent life. But there were of course good wives and bad wives and so in Proverbs 12:4 we read: 'A good wife is the crown of her husband, but she who brings shame is like rottenness in his bones.' As we saw in connection with children, the behaviour of each member of the family reflects on the others. A good wife is recognized for her worth, but a bad one is the cause of much distress to the beleaguered husband. A good wife also attests to the husband's shrewd judgement in choosing her and 'crowns' her husband in enabling him to attain the fullness of his stature and dignity in society, the crown being a symbol of the highest honour as worn by royalty. The definition of a good wife would presumably include her skills at household management, as well as her skills in relationship to her husband and the education of her children. A bad wife, however, is like an inner canker to the bones of her husband, like a fatal disease causing physical and mental distress. Of course it was the mindset of the time to calculate the value of a woman in relation to the male – nowadays we might apply all of these remarks to good and bad husbands!

Proverbs 19:13–14 reinforces the point about each member of the family having an impact on the others: 'A foolish son is ruin to his father, and a wife's quarrelling is a continual dripping of rain. House and wealth are inherited from fathers, but a prudent wife is from the Lord.' Many of us will know from experience just how tiring and draining arguing can be! Of course, it takes two to make an argument which is not explicitly stated here! However, no husband wants an argumentative wife. Whether or not a person will inherit property is an accident of birth, but a thrifty, intelligent wife cannot be inherited – she is a gift from God. Is this divine providence or just a sigh of relief on the part of the husband?! Gaining an inheritance does not involve a personal decision by the husband, but the decision to marry, even if it is an arranged marriage, does and so is more of a risk.

This theme of a contentious woman is repeated a few times in Proverbs – it was a subject close to the heart of the wise! So we read, 'It is better to live in a corner of the housetop than in a house shared with a contentious woman' (Prov. 21:9; see also 25:24). One sometimes comes across couples who have learned to make their marriage work by giving each other a good deal of personal space. In some ways it seems a shame that they don't get on in the way that they once did but, on the other hand, it perhaps means that they are each renewed by some time alone. Some people need this more than others. Clearly the writer of this proverb felt the need to get away to a corner of the house! It would actually have been an uncomfortable, inconvenient and possibly even dangerous option to spend the night on the roof, but the sentiment is that any privation with peace is preferable to the luxury of one's own home with strife. The 'woman' in this proverb may not in fact be his wife – it could be any woman in the house, perhaps his mother-in law! This maxim would of course be equally applicable to an autocratic and quarrelsome male, whose wife might prefer a night on the roof! Proverbs 21:19 goes even further and states that 'It is better to live in a desert land than with a contentious and fretful woman.' This is perhaps too extreme! However, it is true that bad feeling and a bad atmosphere pollute a home so that the desire to escape becomes ever more compelling. Clearly fear of domestic unhappiness weighed heavily with the wise.

There is a long and famous passage in Proverbs 31:10–31 on the benefits of a good wife which actually concludes the whole book. This wife seems to do a great deal beyond the call of normal wifely duty. She manages the household like a business and seems even to have her own money which enables her to make purchases as large as a field. She is kind to the poor and needy and is a skilled needlewoman. She is wise and works extremely hard, getting up early to finish her tasks. She is immensely capable and demonstrates the real rewards that good behaviour, kind deeds and a good relationship can bring. She shows all the benefits of the right choice of wife. The antithesis of the good wife is the adventuress or adulteress or loose woman who is mentioned indirectly at the end of this passage in a reference to charm and beauty, attributes which are so often used as weapons by women but which also accompany the wisdom of the good wife. This reinforces the idea of the two paths, which as we have seen, is one of the main themes of the book – either the young man can find himself a good wife or he can go down the path of sexual licentiousness and short-term excitement. There are many choices to be made in life and this is one of them. It is clear on which side of the fence the Wisdom writers stand.

Friends and neighbours

> Everybody needs good neighbours . . .
> (theme song to *Neighbours*)

Friendship is a great gift because it is freely given on both sides and in true friendship neither side stands to gain more or less than the other. We choose our friends, or they choose us! Discovering who your true friends are is an important issue and being a good friend yourself is a hard undertaking. Unlike family who will put up with a certain amount of bad behaviour, friends are more sensitive and need to be handled with care. In fact we would do well to afford the same level of respect to our loved ones and families that we give to our friends. When it comes to our neighbours, there is a greater element of chance: they may or may not become friends. Whichever way it goes, however, we have to live alongside a neighbour and so it is as well to tread carefully!

We read in Proverbs 17:17 that 'A friend loves at all times, and a brother is born for adversity.' A friend is loyal and caring at all times while a brother can especially be relied upon in times of adversity. Friends may not in fact give us the support we need through the difficult times. We need only to think of Job's so-called friends who were somewhat unsympathetic and critical of him when he met with adversity. There is a difference of opinion amongst scholars over the interpretation of this proverb. Some interpret it as saying that in a crisis a person can be more sure of a brother since kinship has its own obligations which means that he is more likely to be able to be counted on. Other scholars, on the other hand, take the proverb to mean that the spontaneity of friendship leads to a constancy that outweighs the bond of the relative and that if the friendship survives adversity it is indeed a true blessing. Perhaps the proverb is simply equating the two as equally reliable.

Another proverb seems to suggest that sometimes a brother or sister is not the best person to go to – there is contradiction in the thought of the wise on this matter. Perhaps the point is that brothers and sisters shouldn't be taken for granted and automatically counted on for help in times of trouble but should be shown a great measure of

respect. In fact we know that situations can vary enor-
mously from one family to another. Siblings argue over
matters small and large (cf. Prov. 18:19, 'A brother helped
is like a strong city, but quarrelling is like the bars of a
castle' which emphasizes the contrast between love and
strife), while friends are less prone to argue in a personal
way. The fact that we feel we can take liberties with our
brother or sister shows the strength of the brotherly/sis-
terly bond; if we took the same liberties with our friends
too often, our friendship would probably die. A friend is a
supporter, someone who understands our point of view and
who, without necessarily agreeing with us all the time, will
nevertheless treat us with respect. Old friends can be a
particular support. So we read in Proverbs 27:10: 'Your
friend, and your father's friend, do not forsake; and do not
go to your brother's house in the day of your calamity.
Better is a neighbour who is near than a brother who is far
away.' As well as one's own friends, there are family friends
who have often supported the family over a long period of
time. They have watched a child grow up and understand
the ethos of the family. The wise recognized the value of
nurturing such friends and relying on them in difficult
situations. In this proverb friends are seen as potentially
more reliable than family in a time of crisis. This may vary
from individual to individual, but it expresses the point that
friends can be a great support, and old friends even more
so. A further point is made about distance. Air travel and
telecommunications may have changed things somewhat,
but it is still true that it is easier to turn to someone who is
near at hand than someone who is far away. One of the
important things about neighbours is that, just by virtue of
being so close to hand, they can and do help each other out,
a fact which underlines the importance of cultivating local
solidarity in the community.

Along similar lines we read in Proverbs 18:24: 'There
are friends who pretend to be friends, but there is a friend

who sticks closer than a brother.' Here we have the friend/brother theme again but in the rather different context of the reliability of different types of friend. Some friendships do not prove their worth and are fleeting, but others endure and sometimes become as close as a family relationship. The old saying that 'blood is thicker than water' means that shared blood within a family creates a bond like no other. True as that may be, there is a place for very close friends who can be relied upon for support and understanding. Sometimes we might describe a very best friend as 'one of the family' – we know the person and his or her family so well that they are almost like relatives. This proverb then is contrasting social friends who appear warm and friendly but who are ultimately full of chatter with the friend (in the singular here interestingly, perhaps to denote their rarity) who is a friend for life, a kindred soul, one on whom we can rely and who does not walk away in times of adversity; this type of friend is as close as a brother or sister.

The wise also give us advice about our enemies. We read, for example, in Proverbs 27:6 that 'Faithful are the wounds of a friend; profuse are the kisses of an enemy.' It is certainly true that we can be taken in by the flattery of a person who feigns friendship but then is prepared to stab us in the back in order to further his or her own ends. A true friend stays with us through thick and thin and will even dare to criticize us or say a few home truths which might be wounding at the time but probably spring from genuine concern for our welfare. A word of correction at the right time from a true friend might in fact be very important for us, but false and insincere friendship gets us nowhere. The wise clearly understood the value of a true friend and had profound insights as to the nature of real friendship.

Some friends are only there in the good times: 'Wealth brings many new friends, but a poor man is deserted by his friend' (Prov. 19:4). As we saw when we were considering this theme in the context of money, there is an element of blame placed on the poor person who becomes a liability to his friends by making embarrassing demands for money. However, there is also an issue about the nature of friendship. One of the problems of the rich and famous is discerning who their true friends are. People tend to congregate around the wealthy hoping for a share in the pickings. The converse is also true: when people lose their wealth they may also lose their friends. This may be a good thing if they weren't worth having as friends in the first place! It shows the fickle nature of friendship that is not genuine and lasting. Along similar lines we read that 'Many seek the favour of a generous man, and every one is a friend to a man who gives gifts' (Prov. 19:6). Sycophants and flatterers are the kinds of friends of whom we should beware! There is a hint of a warning not to be overgenerous to one's friends, however much one values them, in case they start taking advantage. Equality is an important factor in friendship – it is important that neither side feels any sense of superiority or dependency patterns may be established which are not altogether healthy.

There is always the danger of gossip. It can be very tempting to repeat the confidences of a close friend to a third party, especially when you are part of a group of friends who all know each other fairly well. There is also a place for charitable silence rather than sniping about something, as Proverbs 17:9 expresses: 'He who forgives an offence seeks love, but he who repeats a matter alienates a friend.' Forgiveness in friendship is essential – sometimes a friend makes a mistake for which he or she is genuinely sorry, and we show our own care for him or her by forgiving and forgetting as far as we can. However, careless gossip spoken once too often will inevitably alienate a friend because it leads to a breakdown of trust. And once trust is gone from a friendship it is very hard to get it back. Perhaps, in the desire to continue a friendship, it is better to leave words unsaid: too many words – harping on a fault or repeating it to others – can ultimately destroy a friendship.

It is important, say the wise, to be neighbourly. Having been thrown together with our neighbours, whether we like it or not, we need to make the most of the opportunities for mutual friendship and support that such proximity entails. The wise were aware that one of the dangers of being too friendly with a neighbour is that he or she may start to encroach on a person's privacy. It is better only to go around to a neighbour's house when invited. Hence, the good advice in Proverbs 25:17–18: 'Let your foot be seldom in your neighbour's house, lest he become weary of you and hate you. A man who bears false witness against his neighbour is like a war club, or a sword, or a sharp arrow.' But we also have a duty to support our neighbours. We must never lie about our neighbour's activities: to do so would be a dirty deed indeed. We should also never take advantage of the proximity of a neighbour's house to invade his or her privacy – unless, of course, we see a terrible crime being committed. Neighbours require respect and good treatment and should not be the butt of tasteless jokes: 'Like a madman who throws firebrands, arrows, and death, is the man who deceives his neighbour and says, "I am only joking!" ' (Prov. 26:18–19). This refers to someone who plays a practical joke by randomly throwing weapons, which could have serious consequences, but then tries to pass it off as a joke or a pathetic excuse. Playing cruel jokes on one's neighbour is not a good idea! And a misused word can be as powerful as a misdirected weapon. We are back to the communication theme again.

Another trick the wise do not recommend is talking loudly so that your neighbour can hear you. This too is an opportunity for deceit: 'He who blesses his neighbour with a loud voice, rising early in the morning, will be counted as cursing' (Prov. 27:14). Again, the proximity means that the loud mouth can be easily heard: by speaking in this way the wily person is endeavouring to lull his neighbour into a false sense of security. This seems to refer to the insincerity of a person with a hearty manner which disguises his evil intent. His neighbour – and perhaps the public at large – will eventually see through his overzealous and persistent affectation of friendship. The wise certainly seem to have been aware of the subtleties of false neighbourliness, as Proverbs 29:5 highlights: 'A man who flatters his neighbour spreads a net for his feet.' Although we all enjoy a little flattery from time to time, we must see it for what it is. Flattery is often a trap from which the flatterer wishes to gain something. We all need to beware of flattery and false friendship from friends or neighbours. In fact much of the advice of the wise about friends applies to neighbours too – the sycophant cannot be trusted.

In conclusion, in a longer section, Proverbs 25:7b–10 speaks about the dangers of conflict with neighbours:

> What your eyes have seen
> do not hastily bring into court;
> for what will you do in the end,
> when your neighbour puts you to shame?
> Argue your case with your neighbour
> himself,
> and do not disclose another's secret;
> lest he who hears you bring shame upon
> you,
> and your ill repute have no end.

We may have disputes with neighbours from time to time. When we do, it is far better to resolve an issue locally, on the doorstep so to speak, rather than to bring it out into the open and into a public arena. Once grievances are aired publicly it can lead to open abuse and betrayal of mutual confidences of which neighbours have knowledge. It is far better to make every effort to get on with one's neighbours than for a situation to spiral out of control. Bad-mouthing one's neighbours does not earn one respect in the community – quite the opposite, it leads to one's reputation becoming sullied. The wise, cautioning against making quick judgements just based on what you see, also advise against going too readily to court and involving others in a personal dispute which can lead to the breakdown of the relationship and unwanted meddling. The wise upheld the right of anyone to argue a case, but believed in dialogue and in keeping confidences. Those who gossip and tell tales will only suffer public disgrace in the end.

Conclusion

All's well that ends well . . .
                                    (William Shakespeare)

The Book of Proverbs is like a map that gives us directions. Life will not always fit the directions exactly – and the world changes as time goes by – but there is much in this rich literature that not only speaks to us today, but also gives us an ethical framework for our lives, should we wish to heed its advice. The accumulated wisdom of centuries has been collected in this short book and we are wise if we heed its instruction and pay attention to the insights it gathers together to guide us. The proverbs have been constantly tried and tested in the context of many historical circumstances and so they represent both tradition and change. As we have seen, a pragmatic view of the world such as the wise advocate has implications for all areas of life. It affects our personal behaviour, our relationships with others, our sense of the divine and our attitude to the natural world. It leads us to question, challenge and change.

The wise men of old voiced perceptions about human nature that are just as true today as they were over two thousand years ago. Just as a moral sense can be seen to unite those of many faiths and creeds, wisdom is accessible to all. We have seen that wisdom begins with experience – our human experience of the world and the wisdom of God as Creator and Sustainer of that world. This starting point has much to say to our modern world in which personal experience and individuality are given a high price and in which God is all too often on the sidelines. Some might regard the Wisdom literature as promoting the kind of humanism that is a threat to belief in God. But I do not believe this to be so because the Wisdom world view sees God as a very real power, who set up the world according to certain rules, but who also allows humans considerable freedom of activity. Wisdom appeals to a general moral sense rather than a set of specific laws and defines God broadly as Creator and Orderer and at the limits of human understanding. He has given humanity purpose in life, responsibility for the world and the gift of life itself. We need in response to fulfil our potential as people, to follow our vocations and to live our lives in meaningful ways. We need to celebrate life's diversity and its mystery. We need also to celebrate God's trust in us and become the right kinds of stewards of his world.

Wisdom represents the cumulative experience of many generations, distilled into pithy, memorable sayings so that they can be remembered easily. They reflect the nitty-gritty of human relationships with one another and with God. The wise offer advice, exhortation, and a profound under-standing of the human psyche. We have seen that the topics of the proverbs are everyday, with advice about money, about communicating with others, about family life and societal values. The wise person can use the maxims of proverbs to steer a path through a baffling set of options.

As Creator and Sustainer of the universe it is God who is responsible for order in the world and it is into that order that we, as individuals and members of society, need to tune. This is relevant in a world in which there is an increased awareness of our responsibilities towards our environment, a greater appreciation of origins and diversity in the world and a desire to preserve and protect nature. The modern reader finds a special resonance in the inter-connectedness of nature and humankind with the drawing of parallels between animal and human life and the linking of the mysteries of nature with the mystery of the Godhead. The way the writers of Proverbs describe and categorize the world of nature and the world of human experience constitutes almost a pre-scientific interest. There is a questioning spirit, an ability to live with contradiction and a constant pushing back of the boundaries in the quest for knowledge and truth.

We have seen how the Wisdom writers believed in the importance of purpose in life and hence of work and how they chastised those who were lazy. They saw wealth as a goal towards which to strive and poverty as the result of laziness. They put a high premium on knowledge – knowledge of the way humans behave and knowledge of the natural world and ultimately of God. They understood the value of simplicity, of successful communication and of living life to the full.

Life was seen by the Wisdom writers as a path to be trodden: choose the right path of wisdom and the way would be smooth; choose the path of treachery and seduction and the way would be thorny and rough. The different paths are characterized in Proverbs 1–9 by the two female figures of Woman Wisdom and Woman Folly. Woman Folly is the seductress, portrayed as a foreign woman or 'other', and her path leads to death. Woman Wisdom, on the other hand, is not simply her counterpart but is described as being alongside God at the creation of the world (Prov. 8:22ff.). She is not simply a choice that one makes, as one might make the wise choice of a good wife. Rather she is bound up with the order of the universe, and the message here is that those who learn her instruction and are prepared to receive her education will reap her benefits to the full and will be both at one with the purposes for which God created the world and able to rejoice in following the path to life. This figure of Wisdom is thus at the centre of the conundrum of the meaning of life – she is the word of God on offer, calling out to those who are wise enough to follow her path to know the way to God, to know the way to true understanding and to take delight in life itself.

The world of the wise is in the here and now, a world to be made the most of and enjoyed. Life is essentially perceived as good and as worth living. Their approach is to see everything in terms of what human beings can achieve, to praise human nature and also to see its bad sides. In the main the Wisdom writers relied on experience; they trusted their own judgements and those of others. There is a link up with today's world in this approach in that we tend to trust our own experience more than what others tell us and especially more than the status quo as dictated by institutions. When we are young we learn much from the experience of our parents and teachers, but as we grow to maturity we learn to trust our own judgements above those of others. The wise trusted their experience but their minds were not closed to new ideas; they were prepared sometimes to modify their opinions as new experiences came along. In our own world opinions are constantly challenged and tested and yet there are certain truths that weather the storm of changing public opinion. There will always be a wide range of viewpoints and our task is to steer the right path for ourselves through this maze. The Bible contains unchanging truth of this nature – in Proverbs there is an authoritative body of wisdom that many would benefit from following – and yet if it is to continue to have relevance in the world it must itself be subject to reinterpretation in new contexts.

Whilst they see the bad side of human character, the wise do not see humans as inherently sinful: in fact the whole goal of the Wisdom teaching is to exhort people to change and improve their life. There is in fact an optimism about what human beings can achieve and do for others. They advocate making the most of our lives and interacting in meaningful ways with the lives of others. The wise were concerned with the well-being of the individual, but they were also aware of the need to help others – being responsible in the community by playing one's part to the full in the maintenance of justice and in proper channels of communication.

The wise realized that what you sow you reap. You may think you have got away with something but there will be inevitable repercussions. Moral decisions are not easy – you may be acting within the bounds of your acceptable behaviour where in fact you have offended someone by crossing boundaries acceptable to him or to her. Within any society we need to have conventions so that we all know roughly what those boundaries are. They are instilled into us from a young age and our consciences tell us when we are crossing the lines. Sometimes it is worth the risk of stepping a little over the line – great movements for change have often been started by people who are prepared to step across accepted society lines. It is equally important to live up to the line, i.e. to live life to the full rather than being too afraid to do things or too lazy or unable to face up to difficulties.

Thus wisdom is about self-reliance, bearing the full weight of God's trust and the responsibility which that brings, helping to guide and shape our understanding of human nature and of society at large. We have a responsibility to use our skills to the full for our own fulfilment and on behalf of others. We need not only to cope and to solve our own problems but to be creative in developing our lives and being of assistance to others. We need to rejoice in all the opportunities open to us and not give in when the going gets rough. Life is for celebrating – there is an amazing order in the universe and these patterns can be known to us; there is a spirit of good in the world which hatred and suffering cannot destroy. It is possible to achieve happiness if you walk in the paths of wisdom.